SMART WOMEN
LOVE MONEY

SMART WOMEN LOVE MONEY

FIVE SIMPLE, LIFE-CHANGING
RULES OF INVESTING

———

ALICE FINN

Regan Arts.
NEW YORK

Alice Finn is CEO of Powerhouse Assets LLC, a registered investment adviser firm. The information presented by the author and the publisher is for information and educational purposes only. It should not be considered specific investment advice, does not take into consideration your specific situation, and does not intend to make an offer or solicitation for the sale or purchase of any securities or investment strategies. Additionally, no legal or tax advice is being offered. If legal or tax advice is needed a qualified professional should be engaged. Investments involve risk and are not guaranteed. This book contains information that might be dated and is intended only to educate and entertain. Any links or websites referred to are for informational purposes only. Websites not associated with the author are unaffiliated sources of information and the author takes no responsibility for the accuracy of the information provided by these websites. Be sure to consult with a qualified financial adviser and/or tax professional before implementing any strategy discussed herein.

Regan Arts.

65 Bleecker Street
New York, NY 10012

First Regan Arts hardcover edition, April 2017

Library of Congress Control Number: 2016955002

ISBN 978-1-68245-003-1

Names and identifying details of some of the people and events portrayed in this book have been changed.

Interior design by Nancy Singer
Cover design by Richard Ljoenes

Printed in the United States of America

10 9 8 7 6 5 4 3 2 1

This book is dedicated to the people in my life

who make everything worthwhile—

I love them more than anything.

CONTENTS

SMART WOMEN
LOVE MONEY

INTRODUCTION

Smart Women Love Money—
What Does That Mean?

Love.

We all know what love feels like. When you love people, you love having them around. You take pleasure in nourishing them and watching them grow and thrive. You are committed to them and their well-being, and you want them to achieve their full potential. In a word, you *treasure* them.

Take a moment and think about all that you love in your life. You love your partner or spouse, your children if you have them, your closest family members and friends—maybe even a pet. You might even say you love certain *things*, such as the beach where you and your family spent the summer when you were a child, or a favorite hobby, such as painting or running marathons. Perhaps you'd even say you love your job.

While the feelings you have may be a little different for each of these people and things, you know you love them because you consider them priorities in your life. You carve out time in your schedule to spend with them because you know the time and energy you invest in them will bring about great returns in the form of happiness, stability, growth, and health.

Now, take a moment to consider: when was the last time you felt this way about money? If you're like most women I know, the answer is probably "Never."

When I was brainstorming a title for this book, someone proposed *Smart Women Love Money* and, I'll admit, I cringed a bit. Even as someone who works with money for a living, who helps clients invest their assets precisely so they can have more money in the future, I was fully aware of the emotions most women have when it comes to money. In contrast to the phrase "smart men love money," which seems like a neutral, self-evident statement, saying "smart women love money" evokes a different reaction. Women might *like* money—they like getting a raise or a bonus, saving money by bargain hunting, and having some extra cash set aside for a rainy day—but few, if any, women I know would say they *love* money.

And when it comes to investing and managing money, many women experience emotions much closer to hate or fear. They think they aren't good at math; they don't understand the investment industry and therefore worry they'll get taken advantage of if they get involved; they think it's boring or that, by showing an interest in money, others will consider them shallow or greedy.

After all, when we think about women who "love" money, two images usually spring to mind: the vapid gold digger in pursuit of a rich husband, and the ruthless, unfeeling corporate villain who sacrifices personal relationships in exchange for more, more, more. These stereotypes (and make no mistake, they *are* stereotypes) are completely one-dimensional: women who have sacrificed the truly "important" things in life in exchange for the almighty dollar. In our minds, women who love money *only* love money; there is no room in their lives for anything else.

I didn't want my would-be readers to think this was a book about becoming a money-hungry cliché or that I was saying women weren't smart for valuing relationships, morals, or any other nonfinancial aspect of our lives over the unbridled pursuit of monetary gain. I didn't want women to be turned off by a phrase they found unfeminine, impersonal, or just downright tacky.

But then I had an epiphany. I wanted to write a book about investing—saving, monitoring, and caring for your money in a way that will help it grow over time—that would empower women to make better, savvier, more informed decisions about their financial futures. My hope is that, by reading this book, you will gain the tools you need to retire comfortably, provide for your family well into old age (and even after you're gone), and achieve any goals in the meantime that might currently seem like pipe dreams. In other words, I wanted to write a book about making money a priority in your life—not at the expense of everything you hold dear but *in support* of it. And isn't that what love is?

I wrote this book because I wanted to share with women just how easy (and exciting) it can be when you understand how to invest your money wisely. Given all the chatter, hype, and sometimes panic that surround the world of investing, it's no surprise that women (who have not been socialized to care about money) are wary about dipping their toes into what they see as uncharted waters. But I will show that investing does not need to be complicated or so fraught with emotion. Once you understand the basic rules (which I present as my Five Fundamentals), investing is a relatively painless process that will provide you the resources you will need to thrive not just today but well into the future.

But I also wrote this book because I do want you to learn to love money, not for its own sake but because when you care for and nurture it, you are really caring for and nurturing yourself and the things that are most important to you. Smart women love money because they realize, consciously or subconsciously, that most of us will be solely responsible for our own finances at some point in our lives.[1] They know that even if they work hard and save, any money that isn't earning a return will eventually be depleted (in amount and overall value) due to inflation and myriad future events they cannot predict. They know that even if they are happily married, gainfully employed, and have a supportive network of family and friends, they might not always be able to rely on others to bail them out in case of an emergency. They know, therefore, that it makes sense for them to want to understand how best to oversee the management of their own money, to be responsible for their own investment portfolios, and to be engaged in ensuring their own financial security.

Most women are smart when it comes to the day-to-day decisions about how to earn, spend, and save money. We hunt for the best consumer deals and save up for big expenses such as a family vacation or a down payment on a house. Many of us are even working to close the gender wage gap by negotiating higher salaries on par with what our male counterparts earn.

But too many women are reluctant to focus on the long term and the big picture. In contrast to men, women seem to be wary of becoming involved in the overall management of their personal finances and investments. A 2015 survey by investment firm BlackRock found that of the 4,000 Americans polled, only

53 percent of women had begun saving for retirement, compared to 65 percent of men. Women's average savings were less than half those of the men surveyed ($34,900 versus $76,800).[2] Meanwhile, Vanguard, one of the world's largest mutual fund organizations, reported in mid-2016 that the average balance for women's 401(k) retirement accounts was $75,771, while men's 401(k) accounts contained an average of $115,835, a difference too large to be explained by the gender wage gap alone.[3]

And despite having been born into a world in which we have the freedom to pursue pretty much any career, start our own businesses, and independently manage our own money (a privilege women have had only since 1974, when the Equal Credit Opportunity Act gave them the right to apply for credit without having to have a male cosign), younger women aren't taking full advantage of their rights to invest for their future. A 2014 Wells Fargo study found that while 61 percent of millennial men had begun accumulating retirement portfolios, only half of millennial women had done so.[4] This is worrisome because while women tend to earn less than men—meaning it's more difficult for us to save in the first place—our life expectancy is longer.[5] So a woman's investment nest egg needs to be larger and/or work harder over the course of her lifetime if she wants to be financially secure in retirement.

Why is this? Why is it that women have made strides in so many other areas and yet still have a blind spot when it comes to managing our own money? Admittedly, there are some very tangible obstacles confronting women who try to become financially successful. They may be in a field such as teaching, nursing, or social work that are dominated by women, where they can't parlay their education and skills into the kind of high earnings men with similar credentials might earn in male-dominated professions or jobs. A woman may have taken the "mommy track" in order to raise children and now find that employers subtly discriminate against her when it comes to determining promotions, bonuses, and work assignments.

But there are also many myths and misconceptions that surround our relationship with money—pernicious ideas that get in the way of our better judgment and keep us from making the decisions that will ultimately allow us to thrive. You may not be able to prevent the gender discrimination that has led to your making a lower salary than a male peer. Nor, even if you want to, can you single-handedly reverse the cultural trends that have rendered mothers and daughters the primary caregivers to their young children and elderly parents, giving us little choice but to take time away from our jobs and therefore end up with fewer automatic contributions to our retirement accounts and Social Security. But you can take the steps to combat the myths about women and money—in your own mind and in society as a whole—by educating yourself, learning how to invest wisely, and building a portfolio that will provide you the resources to live a productive and secure life for years to come. In fact, because of the myriad factors that cause women to earn less than men over their lifetimes, it's all the more imperative that we make what money we do have work for us as much as possible. This book is the first step in doing just that.

Women and Money: It's Complicated

In the late 1960s, psychologist Matina Horner, then a PhD student working on her thesis, conducted a study in which she told participants a story about a fictional struggling medical student and asked them to describe the outcome of the character's life. Horner told male participants a story about a character named John, while she gave female students the story of Anne. Horner found that 65 percent of the females described negative outcomes for Anne and had concluded that professional success for Anne would bring about negative consequences in her personal life in the form of social rejection, criticism, and alienation.

To describe this phenomenon, Horner coined the now-famous term "fear of success." "Once [women] could walk through doors that previously had been closed to them," Horner (who later became the president of Radcliffe College at Harvard and was my thesis adviser in college) says today, "They encountered on the other side of those doors unanticipated negative reactions and consequences that they had never before experienced. Previously, the costs of not using their talents had been obvious. But now there were new costs to pay. . . . As more [women] made it into nontraditional arenas, the realities of the negative consequences they faced became evident. They developed their expectations by observing and experiencing the real world." Consequently, women learned to fear and therefore avoid success in areas where achieving success is generally perceived as unfeminine or requiring "too high a price." In contrast, the men in Horner's study perceived achieving success in these areas as having nothing but positive consequences for all aspects of their lives.

The same stereotypes are at work when we think of women and money. Women are socialized to be likable, to be nurturing. And despite the fact that money is a gender-neutral tool we all use to provide for ourselves and our loved ones, caring about money just doesn't jibe with our ideas about femininity. You're probably already familiar with the research that shows women who ask for raises are not only less likely to receive them than their male colleagues but are also more likely to be vilified by their bosses in return—labeled bitchy, aggressive, and demanding while men are regarded as assertive and smart for asking to be paid what they think they deserve.[6]

This stereotype plays out in many ways. Writing recently in the *Harvard Business Review*, Whitney Johnson, professional investor turned management thinker, told a story about a friend who decided to make her new enterprise a nonprofit instead of a for-profit business. Why? "Because women were willing to make donations hand over fist, but they wouldn't invest," Johnson wrote.[7] Admittedly, these were probably affluent women who could afford to pass up the prospect of some investment returns, but why would they prefer to give money away rather than earn a return on a bright idea? It's irrational—until you consider that women are still taught, from an early age, that giving is good and demanding something in exchange is somehow not quite "nice."

Meanwhile, old-fashioned notions about gender roles still play into our approach to money. In her seminal book *The Feminine Mystique*, Betty Friedan chronicled a frustrated generation of women who, despite being well educated and capable, had been coaxed into relinquishing anything other than the most "feminine" roles of wife, mother, and housekeeper. By contrast, during this era, the man of the house fulfilled the masculine duties of earning a living and providing for his family. Money, therefore, was a man's domain.

Of course, modern women have seized back their independence, and the vast majority would laugh at the idea of being told what is or isn't "feminine" in terms of their work and lifestyle. Regardless of whether or not they are married, most women work—indeed, most families cannot afford to live on a single income—and many bring home healthy salaries. In fact, 38 percent of women in heterosexual marriages earn more than their husbands.[8] Ever in pursuit of greater equality in the world and at home, they ask their husbands to share the burden of child care and other responsibilities; compared to their mothers and grandmothers, many succeed at achieving this balance.

And yet, compared to men, women in general take little to no interest in their family's long-term financial well-being. One study by global financial services company UBS found that 99 percent of men and 92 percent of women say they share "overall" financial decision-making with their spouses. But on delving into the details, the bank found that most respondents meant they talked about and agreed on day-to-day financial matters, such as paying bills or making purchasing decisions. When it came to the *investment* decisions, the results were quite different. Half of all couples viewed investing as solely the man's responsibility—and that percentage didn't change much from older to younger couples.[9] That means the men in these couples are single-handedly deciding what life insurance products to buy, how much to set aside for retirement funds and how to invest it, and other long-term financial-planning decisions—even though both partners will have to live with the consequences. (One female engineer acquaintance of mine explained to me that because her husband was handling the family investments, she did not want to learn about investing because she thought it would imply she was worried he wouldn't always be there to handle the investing; she didn't want to educate herself on financial matters because she thought it would jinx her husband's chances of living a long life!)

Because of these gender stereotypes, women are often reluctant to identify themselves as investors and don't fully understand what it means to be one. A 2015 survey by BlackRock found that while 94 percent of women had personal goals that required money to achieve, only 28 percent described money as being an important priority for them. Only a third of those who were investing made the connection between their decision to begin doing so and the fact that putting their money to work in this way would bring them closer to achieving those personal goals. Meanwhile, even though many of them had started putting money away in various investments, a mere 22 percent were willing to describe themselves as "investors."[10]

Another study, commissioned in 2016 by the investment app Stash Invest, found that 79 percent of millennial women believed investing was "confusing." Even worse, 60 percent of them couldn't see themselves in the role of investors. In their eyes, a typical investor was an old white man.[11] When we think of investors, we think of men in suits shouting on the floor of the New York Stock Exchange, or Jordan Belfort, the party-loving stockbroker portrayed by Leonardo DiCaprio in *The Wolf of Wall Street*. Even if we have investments—such as a retirement account—we don't think of ourselves as investors. In actuality, an investor is anyone who puts money to work hoping to get a financial return. That means anyone who has money in a retirement account—e.g., a 401(k), IRA, 403(b), etc.—or in any account that is invested in the stock market and/or in bonds, is an investor, as is anyone who invests in a private company hoping to get a financial return. In other words, most women actually are investors, whether they think they are or not!

As disheartening as I find this statistic about women's

inability to conceptualize themselves as investors, I can't blame women for thinking this way. Society pays lip service to the idea that being prudent in your spending and saving for retirement is a good thing, but advice on how to invest sensibly, and stories about the rewards that come from that, never seem to get much attention. Even when *Glamour* magazine profiled "American Women Now, 50+ Powerhouses" in its September 2016 cover story in an effort to demonstrate the sheer diversity of their interests, activities, backgrounds, and career paths, not a single one of these powerhouses—women the magazine described as "ambitious, outspoken, unstoppable"—worked in finance or even mentioned being an investor.

Even some of our most high-profile and high-powered female role models have succumbed to this thinking. With her 2013 bestseller *Lean In*, Sheryl Sandberg, the chief operating officer of Facebook—who has an estimated net worth of more than $1 billion—became one of the leading advocates for women in the workplace, urging them to embrace new challenges and opportunities as a way to combat inequality. But before the tragic death of her husband in May 2015, Sandberg had spoken about how she ceded control of the family's finances to him as part of their 50/50 division of responsibilities. In 2013, when asked by *Time* about her net worth in the aftermath of Facebook's initial public offering, she ducked the question by implying only her husband knew the answer. "He manages our money," she said. "I have essentially no interest."[12]

I almost fell off my chair reading those words in the magazine I had picked in a doctor's waiting room. Admittedly, Sandberg had the luxury of being able to have no interest. Even after her husband died, she could recruit plenty of financial advisers to step in; any mistakes wouldn't leave her and her children destitute. But conveying the idea of being "uninterested" in money—however honest—was an unfortunate message to send to thousands of women who admire her. Most women simply can't afford to emulate that nonchalance and risk jeopardizing their financial futures.

Achieving Financial Equality through Investing

Unfortunately, in both my personal life and my professional life, I have encountered too many women (even some who have earned MBA degrees from top universities) who, like Sandberg, seem to lack any interest in or engagement with investing. Many women either delegate the investing to the men in their lives, or else they don't invest enough. Perhaps they have some savings and maybe even a tax-sheltered investing account such as a 401(k), but they often leave too much sitting around in cash, uninvested and not earning a return.

This is why I started my company, PowerHouse Assets. After spending the early part of my career in corporate law (a job I was, to say the least, not passionate about), I found my career passion and cofounded an independent wealth-management firm that grew to have billions of dollars under management. While I found this career much more fulfilling, I also started looking for ways to help even more people. By this point I had noticed it was mostly men who were coming to me for advice. Too many women were not paying enough attention to their investment portfolios, leaving them at a high risk for ending up with too little to live on later in life, or at risk of having to start overseeing their investing when a crisis arose—

usually not a good time to have to learn something important and completely new. (A couple of years ago, a friend's elderly father suffered a terrible accident and was not expected to live much longer. He and his wife were concerned how the wife would oversee the family finances as the husband had always handled them, so I paid an emergency visit to them to allay their fears. I was glad I was able to help. However, it would have been much better for the family if this had been addressed before there was a crisis.)

Whenever I could, I involved women in the discussions about financial planning and investing. Involving both partners in a heterosexual couple was beneficial to both parties for many reasons. For one, it helped the woman feel empowered about managing money while simultaneously relieving the full burden of financial planning from the shoulders of the man. You wouldn't buy a house or a car or enroll the kids in private school without consulting your spouse or partner. Why would you make decisions that could affect your entire family's future without doing the same?

I also noticed the traditional investment industry could be off-putting and even discriminatory to women, and I was not alone. When Sallie Krawcheck, one of the top female financial executives in the country, worked at Citigroup and Merrill Lynch in the early 2000s, she monitored brokers to ensure they were speaking to both partners in a couple. Interviewing the brokers afterward, she would ask how much time each had spent talking with each spouse. A broker might say he spent 55 percent of his time talking to the husband and 45 percent addressing the wife, but when Krawcheck referred him to the tape of the conversation, he'd find he'd addressed 90 percent of his remarks to the man. Not surprisingly, Krawcheck says the firm was losing many recent widows as clients.[13]

This unequal treatment at the hands of the financial industry, coupled with the stereotypes that lead them to believe they don't understand investing or that investing should be handled by men, discourages women from asking the questions necessary to get them the answers they need, because they worry about looking foolish or ignorant if they speak up. In an effort to correct this, my company runs gatherings called PowerHouses, during which women can learn about investing in an informal setting (such as a friend's home) in small groups. My goal in designing these meetings is to make them as relaxed and unthreatening—and as informative—as possible.

The women who attend these meetings learn how very simple it actually is to invest their money, following the same fundamental rules you will read about in this book. But one of the best things they learn is that they aren't alone in the way they handle their investment portfolios. Many women confess for the first time that they don't even open their financial statements. Others acknowledge openly—again, for the first time—the psychological difficulty they have in investing the cash that has been accumulating in various accounts (often for years) and their fear that the market will go down after they finally act. Most admit the dizzying array of investment products—mutual funds, ETFs, discount brokerages, etc.—leaves them feeling bewildered and overwhelmed, so they don't know where to start. Some say the prospect of spending time on investing seems boring, that they'd much rather spend their time doing things that are more "fulfilling" or fun. Almost all say they feel too busy to make their own investing a priority, so they never get around to it. Money, which should be their ally— the means by which they can secure their futures and open a world of opportunity—has instead become a source of anxiety.

Each of these women, individually, is very smart and talented. But many of them show up to a PowerHouse gathering because they know they have a blind spot—a lack of understanding about what investing is and how it works—that hampers their ability to invest wisely. Thankfully, this financial blindness is always curable, although the sooner it's treated, the better. In fact, women who attend a PowerHouse always tell me they wish they had focused on their investing sooner (to which I always reply that it's better to start focusing today than it is to wait another day). They also realize that investing is not boring. For example, one woman told me, "It was the best two-hour meeting I've ever been to!" Another said, "It was really great to see women excited and interested in money but more importantly not dreading the thought of it." Even years after women have come to a PowerHouse, they remember what they learned, and it changes their perspective on investing: women realize they must get their money working for them in a way that makes sense—the sooner the better, because money that is not invested has an opportunity cost, and will lead to opportunities lost.

· · ·

Through these PowerHouses, I have seen firsthand how presenting women with simple, straightforward information about investing can transform the way they think about their money and instill in them the knowledge and confidence necessary to take more control of their financial destinies. But as satisfying as it is to host these small, intimate gatherings and to work with these women directly, I believe we have to do more. Too many women have been shut out of the investment industry, not because they aren't allowed in (while discrimination certainly exists, there are no legal or physical barriers preventing women from opening investment accounts) but because our culture and society have led them to feel they don't belong. They've been taught that money is a man's game they aren't suited to play. We've seen how individual women succumb to these stereotypes by saving less for retirement or turning a blind eye to long-term financial decisions. But it goes deeper than that; this financial blindness—and the inequality that results from it—leaves *all* women behind. While we have made great strides over the past several decades in advancing women's equality—fighting for fair pay and equal opportunities, calling out sexism and discrimination when we see it, and encouraging our sisters and daughters to chase their dreams with the same confidence our brothers and sons do—we have largely ignored the very real consequences that come when we don't embrace the role of financial steward and investor.

This baffles me. After all, you might need a boss to sign off on a raise, and who knows how long it will take for our government to be comprised of as many women as men? It might be a long time before we close the gender wage gap or pass legislation to guarantee paid maternity leave or elect a female president. But you don't need to wait for anyone else's consent before you get more engaged in your financial future. You don't need to ask permission to invest your money (even if you don't have that much to start with) in a way that will help ensure you have enough to live on when you get older and, hopefully, even enough to pass on to your children and grandchildren so they can go to college, pursue their own goals, and feel secure as they learn to manage their own finances.

Because women still are reluctant, unwilling, or unable to relinquish their inhibitions regarding money and investing, and accept it is possible—and even responsible—to love money, they still haven't achieved financial parity with men. Until the idea of women loving money is no longer so emotionally fraught, too many women will remain on the sidelines, failing to put their money to work for them by investing it. And as long as women postpone taking on this responsibility for investing their money and securing their future, they won't be financially equal to men. How can women achieve full equality if they haven't reached financial equality?

Perhaps you're now thinking about the women in your family. Perhaps you have a mother or grandmother who married young, never worked, was widowed in her seventies or eighties, and is now living a perfectly comfortable life on her late husband's pension, savings, or other investments. And perhaps you will end up exactly the same way—you'll marry well, your spouse will be a savvy investor who lives a nice, long life and leaves you and your family with a nice nest egg to take care of all major expenses and then some.

But the statistics aren't in your favor. As many as nine out of every ten women will be solely responsible for making all financial decisions for themselves at some point in their lives, even if they do marry a man they believe now shoulders that task. This applies even to happily married women: the rate at which women are widowed is twice that of men, according to government census data.[14] Women who don't marry at all are a growing number: a record 46 percent of American adults younger than 34 are single, having never married, a figure that rose 12 percentage points in only a decade.[15] Meanwhile, women in same-sex couples might find themselves even harder pressed to save enough money for their later years given that both partners may be vulnerable to the stereotypes about women and money. Women in America are still 35 percent more likely to be poor than men,[16] and while the reasons for this are complicated, a contributing factor is that women have smaller investment portfolios.

Women can make great progress financially if we take the higher earnings that our changing work culture has made possible for a growing number of women (if not yet for all) and investing them to secure our financial future and make possible an array of other choices and opportunities decades down the line. Too few women take that step. Even if they're aware of the gender pay gap, financial blindness leaves them oblivious to the gender investment gap and its consequences for them. If we fail to move the dial on this problem, it could end up costing individual women tens of thousands or even millions of dollars over the course of their lifetimes. For those at the lower end of the wealth spectrum, it could spell the difference between comfort and poverty in their old age. For those who are affluent, it means whether or not they will be able to create a personal legacy, philanthropically or otherwise.

I think finance is feminism's final frontier, which is why I wrote this book: to share the knowledge I have used with my clients so all women have the tools they need to achieve financial freedom and maximize their life's opportunities and choices. As I guide you to that frontier in the chapters that follow, and show you how straightforward it can be to oversee how your money is invested, I hope you'll also contemplate the bigger journey you can undertake: from a fear or wariness of money to a love of it, or at least a love of what it can do for you and the ways in which it can empower you.

Don't let factors that are somewhat or completely beyond your control hold you back from investing for your future. The state of the economy will vary; the job market will be more or less healthy than it was last year; our life spans will differ, as will the length of our careers and our earning power; the investment returns we can generate at various points in time will be wildly different. But we can control how we respond to each of these factors, and above all, we can ensure we are proactive in seizing opportunities and managing risk. Because there is a lot at stake.

A Guide to This Book

This book is for all women who want to learn the basic principles of investing so they can put their money to work for them— whether you already have some investments but aren't sure if you're managing them as efficiently as you could or you don't know the difference between a stock and a bond and are just starting to put money into a retirement account. You can learn to invest no matter what your income level. I recognize that if you are in a lot of debt or living paycheck to paycheck, you may not be in a position to start investing right now, but I will walk you through what you need to do to get started on the investment path. As I'll show, the beauty of investing—as opposed to leaving your money in cash in a regular savings account—is that it allows your money to work for you, to earn more money in a way that grows your assets even when you're not paying attention. And over the long haul, this strategy can prove more effective and efficient in growing your money than years of raises or promotions.

In the next several chapters, I'll walk you through the same strategies I use with my individual clients and share with those who attend PowerHouse gatherings. By the time you've finished reading, you'll be ready to take $1,000, if that's what you have at your disposal today, and begin investing. And if you already have millions in your portfolio, you'll learn how properly overseeing your investing can make your portfolio grow even more. Because every day that your money is working for you by being invested properly is a day closer to the financial future you dream of.

Once you've read, learned, and digested the Five Fundamental Rules, you'll be pretty much equipped to venture out and start investing your money or properly overseeing someone else who does it for you. Then I'll walk you through how to start implementing the Five Fundamentals and discuss what questions you need to be sure to ask. I also warn you about certain investment products that may sound great but usually aren't worth the trade-offs you'll make in terms of higher fees and/or a skewed portfolio.

We are on a journey together, you and I, and I'm your guide. I'm going to give you the information you need to reach your destination: the point where you can love money because you now realize what it can do for you and how it can empower you. My hope is that by the end of this book you will realize that loving money does not make you selfish or greedy or unfeminine. It makes you smart. It makes you strong and resilient. And it enables you to take charge of your life in a way that, up until the last century or so, women were not really able to do.

If you're still uncomfortable with the idea of loving money, then think about it in a different way. Think about all the things having more money would allow you to *do*. Have you ever dreamed of starting your own business? Switching to a lower-paying but more fulfilling career? Paying for your children's education so they won't have debt when they graduate, or going back to school yourself? Having enough money to help out your elderly parents if they need help? Taking time off to volunteer or to campaign for a political candidate, or run for office yourself? Becoming a philanthropist and donating a significant portion of your money to a cause you hold dear? Traveling the world with your family so you can expose yourself and your children to new cultures and ideas? Investing can help you do all those things.

Because women have not been encouraged to invest their money properly, so many of them have adopted a mind-set that prevents them from seeing their money's true potential. In 2006 writer and publishing executive Liz Perle published a book— *Money, a Memoir: Women, Emotions, and Cash*—that explored the tangled psychological relationship women have with money. In it, she introduced an analogy of a lake and a river to describe the different ways men and women approach money. Women, she argued, tend to view money as a lake—a finite resource that is capable of being drained dry. Men, on the other hand, see it as a river, constantly being replenished by various sources. The perception that money is a lake inevitably produces anxiety. If money is a finite resource, and is only replenished (from earnings, say) very slowly, it's not surprising that stress will follow.

Every time you pay a bill or make a purchase, you're left counting the diminishing number of dollar bills left in your wallet, and worrying about how long they will last. Even if you make a regular salary, you know one disaster—loss of your job, a medical emergency—could drain you dry in an instant.

Someone who is an investor, however, has a completely different mind-set with respect to money. It doesn't just exist on its own, as a lake does, but it is constantly being replenished. Like a river flowing from its source, money keeps on flowing to you. If you need to dip into it, you don't need to worry that the source will dry up, because your investments will continue to produce returns. There's a source—your investments—and that source just keeps on producing returns.

I have seen this shift in mind-set—from a lake to a river—work a remarkable change in the view women have of money; I've also seen it visibly reduce the level of anxiety they experience when they have to deal with financial matters. One Power-House colleague told me she and a friend came up with a rule: they would no longer obsess about small bills and expenses and would instead focus on how to make money by earning and investing. (In her case, "small" meant less than $250, though of course that number will be different depending on your financial situation.)

By reading this book, I hope you will start thinking about money as a river not a lake, and see how this mind-set shift can unlock a vast new potential for your money—and for you. I hope money stops becoming a source of anxiety or confusion and instead becomes an ally in your quest to achieve the future you hope for. So let's get started.

(1)

THE FIVE
FUNDAMENTALS
Why Investing Doesn't Have
to Be That Complicated

Hopefully I convinced you to become more engaged in your financial future. But I imagine you might still be wary about the logistics. Are you intimidated by the vast array of financial products—stocks, bonds, ETFs, mutual funds, etc.—on the market? Does trying to parse the information coming at you from financial advisers, market experts, or pundits on CNBC stress you out? Are you a former English major who assumes you just don't have the math skills necessary to be good at investing? Even if you have started investing—perhaps your company offers a 401(k) to which you make regular contributions and benefit from an employer match—you might not fully understand the financial statements you receive and want to make sure your assets are being managed effectively.

   If any of this describes you, don't worry. Most people—

women *and* men—are daunted by the investment world, even those who already invest. Here's a secret: investing doesn't need to be that complicated, and much of what makes it appear that way is just noise—a series of distractions, in many cases designed so advisers, brokers, and pundits can charge high fees, push unnecessary products on which they earn a commission, or pedal confusing information that justifies their existence. One client recently came to me with a brokerage statement that was ninety-four pages long! When was the last time you read anything ninety-four pages long that wasn't a book? And the worst part? When I reviewed the statement, I found pages and pages of individual stock positions that had no recognizable strategy behind them. This would make anyone feel overwhelmed and, unfortunately, this is not unusual.

Meanwhile, the constant hand-wringing over the stock market's every move can be enough to make you throw your

---

A traditional broker is a person who executes trades (of stocks and bonds, for instance) on an investor's behalf or sells the investor a product. In return, the broker receives a commission. An adviser, on the other hand, is not paid on commission but only receives a fee from the investor directly in the form of a percentage of assets. This distinction is important because, as we will discuss later in the book, if a large portion of the broker's salary comes from third-party commissions, he or she might have an incentive to make a trade or sell a product that is not in the client's best interest.

hands up in the air. Turn on CNBC, and what do you hear? One pundit says oil prices are going up while another predicts they are bound to collapse. A hotly worded debate follows during the next three minutes and twenty seconds. Then, after a commercial break, it's on to the next topic. Odds are you don't feel any better informed, and even if you do, how are you supposed to act on that "intelligence"? Will either of those pundits be around to advise you about what to invest in and how to manage the associated risks? Or to tell you when to sell those positions? Of course not.

The good news is, you don't need their guidance. You can safely ditch the complicated hedge funds, the outsize bets on energy stocks and, yes, even the winning IPO positions. Because there is an alternative that doesn't require you to play golf or go hunting, fishing, or shooting with the guys (unless you enjoy the sports themselves). It won't be necessary for you to decode brokers' jargon, media pundits, or some super secret Wall Street model. Investing can be straightforward; it doesn't need to be impossibly complex and too difficult to navigate without "expert" guidance.

My Five Fundamentals provide a framework not only to help you invest effectively but also to tune out the hullabaloo that makes investing seem more complicated than it actually is. If there is a secret to investing, it's how simple and easy it can be (and conversely, how paying too much attention to the noise surrounding the markets or paying high fees for a fancy new product or someone's "expertise" can actually *hurt* you). Once you understand my Five Fundamentals—and in the next five chapters you will—you will have the foundation for understanding everything you need to know about investing.

So what are the Five Fundamentals? I'll explain each of these in depth in the chapters that follow, but for now, here they are:

THE FIVE FUNDAMENTAL RULES

Rule #1
Invest in Stocks for the Long Run

Rule #2
Allocate Your Assets

Rule #3
Implement Using Index Funds

Rule #4
Rebalance Regularly

Rule #5
Keep Fees Low

As long as you follow these five rules, you will end up with an investment portfolio that will be more effective in managing and growing your money over the long term than expensive, complicated alternatives. I know it can be done, because I have been advising high-net-worth clients since the mid-1990s and generating attractive returns for them from the stock and bond markets with a relatively simple approach. It's been proven to work time and time again, and it enables them to understand and feel comfortable with the process. It also allows me to keep their fees low because I'm not engaging in some super special strategy that needs high-priced gurus or teams of people to execute. In fact, many others in the financial-adviser industry use a similar straightforward, low-cost approach, but unfortunately, most do not.

Moreover, even though I generally use these principles working with wealthy clients, any woman can apply them successfully to her own portfolio and investment strategy. It doesn't matter whether you have a few thousand dollars in a savings account that you are preparing to invest for the first time or if you are trying to manage many millions in a trust bequeathed to you by your well-off family. Together, these five rules will give you a clear vision of your goals and objectives, while reminding you of the best way to accomplish them.

Once you have grasped these principles, you will have the kind of solid foundation you will need in order to go ahead and invest without anxiety, without a sense of constant pressure. Even if you don't understand every product or term you encounter, or still get overwhelmed by the constant chatter in the financial media, you will know enough to ask the right questions, figure out which low-cost products to invest in, and ignore many unwanted distractions.

One of the biggest benefits of learning the Five Fundamentals is that they help you realize just how important it is to put your money to work now, rather than wait any longer. One woman I worked with, Charlotte, is a telecommunications industry manager who lives in the Southeast and had accumulated more than $500,000 in savings that had been sitting in cash for years. Had Charlotte invested that nest egg in a diversified portfolio made up largely of stocks (the first of my Five Fundamentals), over a decade she might have been able to earn an average of 7 percent per year during those ten years—doubling her money during the decade to more than $1 million—based on the kind of returns stocks have produced historically. Sure, Charlotte would have been running a risk; that's what you do whenever you try to earn a good return. But instead she left her money in cash, which guaranteed—based on today's ultra-low interest rates—that she not only forfeited the chance to earn those returns but that inflation was nibbling away at the value of her portfolio. Had she continued on that path, by the time she needed to draw on her savings to support her living expenses in retirement, they wouldn't have been adequate for the task.

But once she grasped the Five Fundamentals, Charlotte understood how she had been short-changing herself and what she needed to do to fix things. She moved her savings to an investment portfolio and is now on track to make that money work for her in the years she has left before retirement.

Other women I've met have sabotaged themselves in more subtle ways. Some confess they don't open the statements they get from their financial advisers, shoving them into a desk drawer where they are left unread. Still others have abandoned their 401(k) accounts after moving on to new jobs, and find that years later, they have no idea how much they have left behind, or what it is invested in—or even where the accounts are now. And if they manage to locate all that money and figure out how much they have in their accounts, they feel paralyzed. What comes next? These situations are amazingly common.

These rules won't work miracles, of course. If you are over-spending, are mired in debt, or are unemployed and struggling to cover your routine expenses and can't set aside money to invest, then obviously you'll need to tackle some of these other problems before you set about saving and investing. But once you have that under control, these are simple, easy rules to follow that will enable you to get engaged in what can be the most rewarding part of your financial life: your investments.

This Is Not a Math Problem

In the introduction, I discussed several of the stereotypes surrounding women and money—that it's unfeminine or a man's job, or that any woman who takes an interest in money will naturally be sacrificing more "important" aspects of her life. But there is another stereotype that might be making you hesitant to move forward: women aren't good at math. And don't you need to understand math to be a good investor?

Honestly, not really. Yes, there are numbers involved, but the actual math you will need to make sense of your portfolio is basic arithmetic: some multiplication, division, and percentages. Sure, the finance industry runs on complicated algorithms that require actual math experts to manage, but you don't need to be a math genius to invest your money wisely.

And before you protest that no, really, you aren't good at math—even the basics—consider that perhaps your lack of confidence is a self-fulfilling prophecy spurred by stereotypes about your gender. For starters, studies have shown that women in some countries, such as Indonesia and Iceland, routinely do better than men at the top tier of mathematical tasks.[1] And while according to some much-contested studies, Caucasian men are better at mathematical tasks than Caucasian women, that pattern is reversed for Asian Americans. Meanwhile, researchers have found that women who are asked to check a box marking their gender before a math exam routinely fare worse than women who check that box after, indicating that perhaps the stereotype that women aren't good at math actually causes them to perform worse at math (a phenomenon that psychologists refer to as stereotype threat).[2]

And even if you couldn't ace a high-level calculus exam, you are likely already much better than you realize at dealing with math when it comes to money. When you go grocery shopping, you've probably caught on to the tricks that food companies play with packaging sizes and learned to comparison shop based on price per ounce in order to get the best deal. If you use a credit card, you understand that the interest you owe compounds on top of any previous interest accrued (a process that can wreak havoc on your credit as it dramatically increases the debt you carry but can do wonders for your investments). And you know how to spread your money across a number of categories in order to make sure all your needs are met, a process known in everyday life as budgeting, and in investing as asset allocation.

It's also worth noting that a study by Vanguard of participants in its defined contribution retirement plan found that men and women did roughly as well as each other over a five-year period: men posted median returns of 10.9 percent, while women's gains were 10.6 percent.[3] That doesn't suggest that women have any inherent deficit in understanding or ability. A separate study, by online investment firm SigFig, found that their female clients actually did better than the men who used the firm's web tools to track their portfolios. They studied both men and women for a one-year period in 2014 and found women outpaced men by 12 percent, earning returns of 4.7 percent compared to 4.1 percent.[4] It seems actual results don't justify women's lack of self-confidence in the investment sphere, or men's abundant self-confidence.

Finally, despite all these reasons, even if you still don't feel confident in your mathematical abilities, the Five Fundamentals don't require you to be. They are foundations, the first steps toward understanding the financial world so you can, with practice, become a confident, successful investor.

What's most important is that you don't let your current lack of confidence stop you from investing in the first place. And if you think it's already too late, it's not. No matter where you are now, you can put your money to work for you today. And as we'll see in the following section, the sooner you start, the better.

The Magic of Compounding

One of the reasons investing can be so intimidating, besides what I already described, is that the dollar amounts discussed are often very large. By the time women turn 65, consultants who advise companies on how to structure retirement packages say most of them should have set aside eleven times their annual earnings if they want to be able to afford their current standard of living after they retire. So if you're making $75,000 before taxes, experts suggest you have a retirement nest egg of $825,000; if your salary is $200,000, the figure should be $2.2 million. Those can be intimidatingly large numbers for someone just starting to save and invest.

My advice: don't focus on the large numbers right now. They are long-term goals, and investing is a long-term process. You may be starting out with $1,000 to invest—or maybe even less if you're young and earning a comparatively low salary—but if you invest that money, as opposed to leaving it in a low-interest savings account, you can make it turn into a whole lot more. And it's all thanks to the magic of compounding.

If you have a credit card or have done some basic research into investing already, you are already familiar with compound interest. You charge something to your card and, if you carry that balance (or a portion of it) over to your next statement period, you have to pay interest on it. If you carry that (now higher) balance over to the following period, you not only have to pay interest on the principal (the amount of your original purchase), you have to pay *interest on the interest*. So if you charge $100 to your card, don't pay it off, and are accruing 15 percent interest, you will then owe $115. If you then fail to pay it off, you will owe $132.25, which amounts to an additional 17.25 percent of your original principal (i.e., 132.25 − 115 = 17.25 and 17.25/100= 17.25%).

This is bad news if you have a lot of credit card debt, but it is great news for investors because compounding works exactly the same way on your investments, except in the right direction—earning you more money on top of your initial investment and compounding it over time. Albert Einstein is said to have described compounding as the eighth wonder of the world, and while this story might be apocryphal, it's pretty hard to disagree with that conclusion. Imagine being able to set aside a few thousand dollars every year, invest it in stocks, and see it become hundreds of thousands over the decades. It's not impossible, thanks to compounding.

Compounding means your earnings and profits go on to generate profits of their own, if you can be disciplined enough to leave them in your portfolio, or "reinvest" them instead of withdrawing them. So if a stock you purchased for $10 rises 20 percent to $12 in year one and rises another 20 percent the next year, that second gain is actually worth more to you in dollar terms, because you're getting not just the gain on your original $10 investment but also on the extra $2 gain, which you reinvested. The more time that passes, the more important these "profits paid out on top of profits" become in your portfolio.

Compounding is truly magical. Let's say you own stocks that pay dividends and grow in value. When you reinvest those earnings so *they* start to earn money for you too, that is compounding in action. For instance, if you invest $10,000 and earn 10 percent in a year, you'll walk away with a profit of $1,000. If you reinvest that, and earn 10 percent the second year, you'll make another $1,000 on your initial investment—plus $100 on the extra $1,000. You keep going like that, adding the profits you make along the way, and over time, the amount of money you can earn thanks to compounding can really add up. In fact, the rule of thumb is that if you're earning about 7 percent a year, and you reinvest in a disciplined way, your money will double every ten years. (Alternatively, if you're earning 10 percent a year, it will take only seven years to double.) Compounding is the seemingly miraculous reward the stock market gives a disciplined investor.

Every year, the prior years' earnings are generating more profits for you, working harder and becoming increasingly significant. After seven years of 10 percent gains, your original $10 investment is now worth $19.49. If, in year eleven, it goes on to earn a 10 percent gain, you'll make 10 percent of $19.49, not 10 percent of $10. Soon your profits will be much more than your original investments.

This is why investing is so much more effective and efficient at growing your money than simply saving it (because most standard savings accounts generate low interest rates) or even earning a higher salary. How often do you receive a 10 percent raise? And even if you do, you have to work every day to earn it. Comparatively, becoming your own personal investor can become the highest-paid per-hour job you could ever have.

One of the common excuses I hear from women who have put off investing is that they are "too busy" to be bothered with it. But once you've determined your asset allocation (a process I describe in detail in chapter 3) and select your investments (chapter 4), all you really need to do is monitor it every few months to be sure all is well, and give your portfolio a once-annual financial checkup. In fact, if you spend a lot of time managing your investment portfolio, I can almost certainly tell you you're doing something wrong. Meanwhile, even when you're not looking, your money will be working for you. This isn't like going to the gym and working out, where the only time you improve your fitness is when you're actively engaged in some kind of physical activity. On the contrary: the beauty of investing is that the returns will keep accumulating while you work, while you eat, while you sleep, while you're on vacation, while you're at the movies with friends. Sure, you'll need to check in on the portfolio from time to time, but it's a small percentage of all the hours you'll spend on other annual tasks you make time for each year, such as doctor and dentist appointments and working on your tax returns.

As I said in the introduction, when we love something, we set aside time for it and make it a priority. You would never say you were too busy for your family or your friends or taking care of your health, so why would you treat money so callously? Thankfully, money is pretty self-sufficient, requiring a small fraction of your attention in order to fulfill its potential.

Don't Be Intimidated. Start Now!

Compounding also explains why it's important to start investing as soon as possible, because the sooner your money starts earning a return, the sooner you can reinvest that return for even greater returns. By the time you've finished this book, I hope you are ready and willing to get started, but if you're still feeling daunted, I have one piece of advice for you: ask lots of questions.

I start every PowerHouse gathering by making sure the women there really grasp this fundamental truth. Even the most basic questions, such as, "What is a stock and what makes it different from a bond?" and "Why does the stock market go up?" are *not* stupid questions.

Finance is one of the only subjects we learn about as adults, and that happens largely through trial and error (consider that as of this writing twenty-four states require that sex ed be taught in high school but only five require that personal finance be taught). That means that by the time we reach the point in our lives where we have money to invest, we tend to be educated in everything we need to know *but* the financial markets. We're knowledgeable when it comes to our jobs, have achieved a certain level of self-confidence in our personal lives, and have mastered all the skills related to daily living. Suddenly, we're confronted with something that's very important to us—and we have no idea how to talk about it. Of course we're going to have basic questions. That doesn't mean they are stupid. In fact, you can be fairly sure that if you're part of a group of people, and you ask what you fear will be a stupid question, it's one that six or seven others in that group are secretly longing to ask but are afraid to. You're not a dolt; in fact, you're a hero for speaking up.

In the chapters that follow, I intend to address some of the most basic questions people have when they start investing. There will still be plenty of questions to ask—especially because everyone's financial situation and goals are different—but my hope is that I will have armed you with enough knowledge to know which questions to ask, to figure out what is worth learning more about and what is simply a distraction.

And as I said at the beginning of this chapter, there will be distractions. But once you make the Five Fundamentals central to your investment process, you'll understand just why the question of whether or not Apple is a "good stock" at its current price is completely irrelevant. You will shrug off the gyrations associated with the arrival on the scene of a "game-changing" world event such as Brexit or the election of Donald Trump. The price of gold or oil? That too is irrelevant. If you allow yourself to be distracted by any of these short-term events, you'll either go crazy chasing what you think is going to happen or fork over as much as half of any of the investment profits you do make to Wall Street advisers—who will try to "time the market" for you, which, as I'll explain later, is essentially impossible to do—in the form of fees.

Keeping your focus on the Five Fundamentals will protect you from the glittering false promises of those on Wall Street who peddle "black box" investments (meaning investors don't really know what's inside). They say these investments are managed using secret formulae they won't disclose but that will allegedly allow you to beat everyone else in the market or magically enable you to earn a steady 10 percent return annually, no matter what the market happens to be doing. That's the kind of extra-special formula Bernie Madoff offered his hand-picked investors—hand-picked for their willingness to refrain from asking probing questions or insisting on common-sense investment strategies. Anyone with an understanding of the Five Fundamentals would have realized immediately there was something fishy about Madoff, even if they couldn't have figured out he was running a Ponzi scheme.

Even if learning these rules won't turn you into a forensic accountant, it should help you develop the instincts of a good investor. Instead of becoming agitated when listening to media pundits debating whether gold will be heading up or down over the next few months, you can relax and see these shows for what they are: entertainment. Pretty much everything being squawked about on *Squawk Box* (or any other entertaining financial program) will not matter to your portfolio in the long run. When a question arises that you think might affect your investment portfolio or strategies, you can test it using the Five Fundamentals. Does a proposed idea or product fit into your asset allocation? If it's a stock product, is it an index fund with ultra-low fees? What are its costs or fees? Who would you be paying, and what would you be paying them for?

For the most part, if an investment idea doesn't fit into the Five Fundamentals, you can ignore it. There's usually no good reason for changing anything or buying any new product that your colleague, best friend, or even your spouse falls in love with. Even if Uber goes public, and you ride in Uber cars all the time, you'll learn that owning a lot of individual stocks—no matter how hot they are—just isn't going to produce the same kind of rational, properly diversified, efficient portfolio that owning index funds will produce for you (the Third Fundamental).

The Five Fundamentals will provide you with the tools to address your basic investment decisions. They will help you construct the kind of plain vanilla investment portfolio that is all you really need to get on the path to investment success. There is no list here of the ten stocks you must own for the next decade, or a key to Wall Street's secret trading tips. Individually these five rules are valuable principles. Together, they are an unbeatable approach for laying the foundation to become a confident, smart investor who loves getting her money to work for her.

2

The First
Fundamental
Invest in Stocks
for the Long Run

There's a scene in the classic film *The Graduate* in which Dustin Hoffman's character, Benjamin, newly graduated from college and mulling his future, is approached by Mr. McGuire, a friend of his parents. In an effort to help Benjamin figure out what to do with his life, Mr. McGuire urges him to consider "just one word . . . 'plastics.'"

When it comes to investing for *your* future, there's a word I want you to keep in mind: "*stocks*."

If you know anything about the stock market, you know it can be extremely volatile. All you have to do is look back to the Great Recession of 2008—not to mention earlier disasters such as the Great Depression of the 1930s—to get a glimpse of what can happen when the market takes a turn for the worse and individual investors are left with a lot less in their portfolios.

But if we take a wider look at history, it's clear that over time stocks are, hands down, the best long-term investment—even when you factor in depressions, recessions, stagnations, and other market disasters. In fact, as I'll explain in this chapter, one of the easiest ways to lose money in the stock market is to react too quickly or too often to fluctuations.

Take a look at the following chart, Figure 2.1.

These squiggly lines tell a powerful story. Those top two lines—the ones that are soaring way above the others—represent how well large company stocks (as represented by the Standard & Poor's 500-stock index or its equivalent in the years before this index existed) and smaller company stocks fared between 1926 and 2016. Look closer, and you'll notice the starting value is $1, which means, if your grandmother or great-grandmother had invested just $1 in large company stocks or small company stocks in 1926, that money would have been worth $6,031 or $20,544, respectively, by 2016. This is true in spite of the fact that the Great Depression would have struck just a few years after she entered the market. If she had gotten out of the market during the Depression, not only would she have lost money by selling her shares, but she would also have missed out on the amazing long-term returns that followed for the next ninety years.

In comparison, if she had opted to invest in a lower-risk investment vehicle such as government bonds, she would have ended up with $134, even though this period includes the last thirty years, which has been one of the biggest rising or "bull" markets for bonds ever known. Interest rates have gone down pretty steadily during this period, from around 15 percent for long-term bonds to the low rates they are today, and as inter-

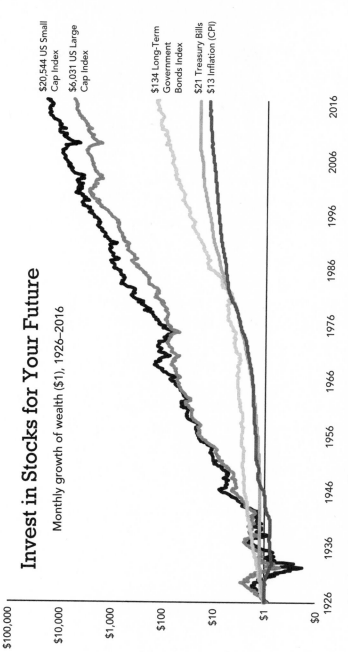

Invest in Stocks for Your Future

Monthly growth of wealth ($1), 1926–2016

- $20,544 US Small Cap Index
- $6,031 US Large Cap Index
- $134 Long-Term Government Bonds Index
- $21 Treasury Bills
- $13 Inflation (CPI)

Figure 2.1

The Standard & Poor's 500 index (S&P 500) is the most popular stock market index, tracking 500 of the largest and most actively traded companies in the US stock market. It was created back in 1923 as a much smaller market tool, with only a few companies, and only in the 1950s did it expand to include 500 stocks. Like all indexes, it is a basket of companies; the company that created, designs, and oversees it, Standard & Poor's, intends investors to use it as an indicator of how the stock market is faring.

When you invest in "the index" you don't literally buy the index itself, but funds other companies build that are designed to replicate all the companies in the index, and that as a result will behave exactly like the index does at any given moment of every day. The companies in the S&P 500 are selected by a committee and must meet certain criteria; the committee's goal is to include the largest public companies but also to represent all industry sectors. The largest companies (such as Apple) have the most impact on the index's movement because the index is weighted by company size. This is in contrast to the Dow Jones Industrial Average, in which each one of the thirty blue-chip stocks included has an exactly equal impact on how the overall index moves, regardless of its size.

est rates go down, the value of bonds goes up (more about this later). Had she put that money in shorter-term government treasury bills (which typically pay less in interest because you're taking less risk with these shorter-term investments), she'd have a measly $21—barely enough to compensate for inflation.

Of course, these lines are jagged lines, not straight ones. That means there were periods in this nearly century-long span when, if you were an investor, you were in for a bumpy ride. During the 1970s, the line goes relatively flat—stock market returns were scarce, and if you talk to an older broker or trader, you'll hear some depressing stories about how tough it was for them during that period. Then there are the glory days. You may remember the mid-1990s, when for several years in a row, the S&P 500 posted an annual return in excess of 20 percent,

Inflation. It's essential to invest your money and not just leave it to lie idle in a savings account, if only to be sure that when you need to draw on it, it will retain its purchasing power. It would be fun to live in 1970 with a 2017 salary, but the reverse—trying to eke out a living in 2017 on a 1970 budget—wouldn't make for such a good time. But that's what you do if you don't pay attention to the impact inflation can have on your savings. Inflation erodes your retirement nest egg unless you earn an investment return that matches or exceeds the inflation rate. So when you're thinking about how much you want to earn from your portfolio, your goal should be to earn a healthy "real" rate of return, with that being defined as the difference between your actual returns and the inflation rate. So if inflation runs at about 2 percent a year, on average, and you make 7 percent, your "real" rate is 5 percent. But if you leave your money sitting in cash and collect nearly nothing on it, and if inflation is 2 percent, then each year you can kiss good-bye 2 percent of your hard-earned savings, in terms of its purchasing power down the line.

while the Dow Jones Industrial Average crossed one 1,000-point milestone after another: Dow 5,000 in November 1995, Dow 6,000 in October 1996, Dow 7,000 in February 1997, and Dow 8,000 in July 1997. There were blips. Some were brief—even though they felt like the end of the world to the stock traders who lived through them—such as the Black Monday of October 1987 when the Dow dropped by more than 22 percent. But other events were far more serious and prolonged, from the Great Depression of the 1930s and the bursting of the dot-com bubble in early 2000 to the most recent financial crisis that began in 2007, which the economy only started to recover from in early 2009, and whose effects are still rippling through the economy and the financial system.

All these have been interruptions to what has been a long-term upward trend, however. And it's that trend you need to keep in mind. If you've been dithering on investing in the stock market because you are worried about taking on the risk, then I hope this chart serves as your wake-up call.

How to Make Money in Stocks

Stock is an ownership interest in a company. One way companies raise the capital they need in order to operate is by selling part of the business, and those ownership interests are known as shares. The investors who buy those shares of company stock—the company's owners—are referred to as shareholders. Most of the country's biggest companies, from General Electric to Facebook, have raised capital through sales of stock to the general public and not just to insiders, such as those who work at the company or friends and family, or from venture capitalists who finance start-ups, etc. Their shares now trade on stock exchanges, where anyone who wants can buy and sell them.

Shareholders can make money in two ways. The first happens when stock prices rise, in what are referred to as capital gains; usually this is where the majority of profits in stocks come from. The second comes in the form of dividends, which are paid out of the company's profits or cash flow, usually on a quarterly basis. Dividends tend to make up a relatively small percentage of returns on stock investments, and only some stocks pay them.

Compounding, which I explained in the last chapter, also explains why stocks are such a wise long-term investment. The value of a stock is determined by market forces—how much people want to buy versus how much people want to sell. Therefore, if there is a big demand for a stock after you buy it, you have a greater chance of earning a higher return. And if that return stays positive over the long haul, you will start to earn returns on previous returns.

Compounding also explains why it's imperative to invest now rather than later. The sooner you get your money into the stock market, the sooner it can start working for you, year after year after year. This is true for all investors, but it's especially important for women, who, as I mentioned in the introduction, tend to live longer but earn lower lifetime salaries than men. You can't afford to sit and brood about past mistakes or fret that you don't know enough about finance to get involved.

Sadly, this happens over and over again. Lucy, a technology industry manager in the Southwest, received a large lump-sum payout from her company to settle a suit she had filed claiming she had been discriminated against in terms of her wages for many years. Lucy felt good about the settlement, but when she got the check, she promptly deposited it in the bank and left it there for years to gather the investment equivalent of dust. In other words, instead of earning an annual return of 7 percent or so, it sat idle, earning almost nothing given that banks are paying a fraction of a percentage point in interest on savings deposits. This story is doubly sad, because after her wages suffered due to her company's discrimination, Lucy's lack of understanding about investing led her to make decisions on her own that hurt her financial future.

No one can predict the future, but as the preceding chart illustrates, history proves that regardless of market turmoil and uncertainty, stocks are the surest way to earn a relatively high return on your investments in the long run—no matter how small your investment is to start. Yes, history may change course and this trend might not continue forever. But what are the odds of that happening in your lifetime? What would it take to reverse the long-term upward trajectory of the stock market?

One question I have been asked (quite depressingly) a number of times is, "What if there's a nuclear war?" It is true that in the case of a cataclysmic disaster, all past patterns will likely be irrelevant. But here's another question: "If something as cataclysmic as a nuclear war happens, are you really going to be worried about your portfolio?" You'll have a lot more to worry about, and you certainly won't be alone. Why not be optimistic and invest in stocks rather than worry about a hypothetical disaster that will wipe out the value of any cash you have "safely" put away anyway?

All the advice I present in this book—the same advice I give to my clients and use in my own personal investing—is based on probabilities. Because no one can predict the future with certainty, the best anyone can do is play the odds that are in their favor. If you look again at Figure 2.1, you should see

A bond, like a stock, is an investment product that is a way for a company (or the government) to raise money. But instead of buying ownership in an entity (like you do when you purchase stock), you are lending money to the entity for a given period of time. Think of it as an IOU. At the end of the lending period, the entity who issued the bond will pay you back your original investment, plus you will have earned interest, the rate for which is set when you first buy the bond if it's a fixed-rate bond. Bonds are generally considered "safer" investments than stocks because your return is guaranteed (unless the company goes bankrupt) and is not based on how well the company performs during the lending period. Bankruptcy laws also stipulate that bond holders must be paid before shareholders, so if the issuing entity gets into financial trouble, you will be more likely to get your money back if you invested in bonds. However, since for these reasons they are considered less risky (unless you are purposely buying risky bonds such as "junk bonds"), the returns are usually lower than what you can expect to see in the stock market. And now, since interest rates are so low and are likely to rise over time, meaning the value of these low-interest-rate bonds will go down in comparison to newly issued bonds issued at a higher interest rate, bonds actually have more risk than during the bond bull market when interest rates were falling and bonds that were issued with higher interest rates became more valuable.

that investing in stocks makes sense. Yes, in the short term you can lose money in stocks, but if you are reading this book, it's because you're concerned with the long term: What are you going to have when you retire? How are you going to finance your lifelong goals? How are you going to provide for your family in your later years and after you're gone? You're not looking for stock tips to help you make a quick buck but a way to reshape the way you think about money that will truly be life-changing.

That means your investment portfolio is—and should be—a long-term project. And the longer your investment time horizon—that is to say, the earlier you invest and the longer you can leave your money untouched and invested—the more important stocks should be to you. As we will explore in the next chapter, that doesn't mean there's no place for other investment vehicles, such as bonds, but simply that they should not make up the lion's share of your portfolio.

Another question I'm often asked is, "What happens if the stock market just stops going up, since it's already so high?" While there have been periods in the past where the market has hit the pause button for a little while, this upward pattern has always resumed. Why? Because when you buy shares of a company, you are betting that company will do well, that they will continue to come out with new and amazing products and services that will make them money. Sure, companies fail all the time, but you will not be investing in just one company (we'll talk more about this in chapter 4); you'll be investing in the market as a whole. Companies whose stocks are being traded don't stop being innovative and productive, and when investors anticipate future profits or those profits actually materialize, investors will eventually buy the stocks, sending the stock prices higher. So unless we all collectively decide to stop being innovative, starting new businesses, inventing new technologies, and designing new products, there will be money to be made in the stock market.

Don't Try to Time the Market

If you've been exposed to any investment advice in your life, you've probably heard phrases such as "Buy low, sell high!" or heard investors brag about how they made millions by selling their shares just before a market crash and then turned around and bought them again after the price plummeted. After all, if stocks are subject to volatility that decreases their value—at least in the short term—doesn't it make sense to try to maximize short-term profits using this strategy rather than weathering the losses?

The way media pundits and investment gurus discuss the market implies that getting in and out of the market this way in order to maximize investment profits is possible: Is it overvalued? Undervalued? Ready for a correction (translation: selloff)? What does the latest development at Apple or General Electric mean for their share price, and should investors in these companies buy or sell shares of the company's stock?

But the reality is that for all their talk and "expertise," people who engage in market timing—as this strategy is called—in order to maximize profits are usually right only about 50 percent of the time, if not less. This of course means they are wrong about 50 percent of the time, if not more. In other words, they are basically guessing.

You have to stay put in stocks to make money. You need to commit to your relationship to the stock market, just as you would to any other relationship from which you hope to benefit over the long run. Yes, on a day-to-day basis, the stock market can be tremendously volatile and nerve-racking. Those big gains in the 1990s? There was at least one year in that period during which stocks simply flatlined, and two periods during which overseas market crises triggered temporary market sell-offs of hundreds of points in the Dow Jones Industrial Average, prompting around-the-clock coverage by overexcited talking heads. Had you responded by selling, odds are you would have missed out on some of the best days in the market. And that would have been extraordinarily costly.

As the following chart (Figure 2.2) shows, let's say you had invested $1,000 in the Standard & Poor's 500 index in January 1970 and left it untouched until December 2015. Your stocks would have produced profits at an annual rate of 10.27 percent and you would have ended up with $89,678! That's not too shabby, especially when you consider that period included a lot of negative events for stocks, ranging from the stagflation of the 1970s to the dot-com bubble burst of the early 2000s and the Great Recession we have just experienced.

However, if you had tried to time the market over those forty-five years and been out of the market on the five days during which the S&P 500 performed the best, you would have been left with only $58,214, or an annual return of 9.24 percent. In other words, had anything caused you to be skittish and sell at the wrong time, you would have cut your returns by a third. And remember, we're talking about missing only five days. Had you missed the twenty-five best days over the course of that forty-five-year period, you would have ended up with only $21,224. If you had missed out on even the single best day, you would have lost out on more than $9,000. That's a big tax on missing the single best day in the market—especially because you can never predict in advance which day that is going to be.

Trying to Time the Markets Can Wipe Out Your Returns

Performance of the S&P 500 Index, 1970–2015

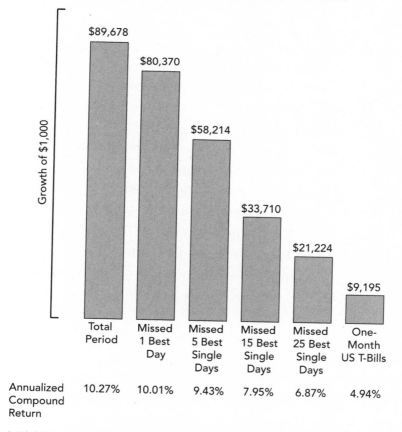

	Total Period	Missed 1 Best Day	Missed 5 Best Single Days	Missed 15 Best Single Days	Missed 25 Best Single Days	One-Month US T-Bills
Annualized Compound Return	10.27%	10.01%	9.43%	7.95%	6.87%	4.94%

Figure 2.2

Now, what are the chances you would miss out on the five or twenty-five best days over a forty-five-year period like this? Surely, the best days would come in the midst of big market rallies, and so you wouldn't abandon ship, right?

Not necessarily. According to a recent study by JPMorgan Chase, during the twenty-year period between 1995 and 2014, six of the ten best days for financial markets were recorded within two weeks of the ten *worst* days. In fact, the single-best day of that forty-five-year period discussed previously was October 13, 2008, during which the S&P 500 went up 11.58 percent—just two weeks after the 8.8% drop on September 29, 2008.[1] What do you think the chances are that, if you had reacted to one of the worst sell-offs in a decade by selling your stocks, you would have calmed down and regained your appetite for risk within two weeks or less? Isn't it much better for both your blood pressure and your portfolio's performance just to stay put, ride out the storms, and profit from that long-term trend?

None of us has a crystal ball capable of warning us which days in the stock market will wreak havoc on our portfolios and then reminding us to jump back in so we can be around on those days when markets will deliver blockbuster returns. In practice, trying to do that leads us to buy high and sell low—and, in the worst cases, participate in the market's biggest down days, and then be frightened out of the stock market and miss out on its biggest one-day upswings. In the words of Charles Ellis, a leading consultant who helps many of the country's largest pension funds make their investment decisions, "Market timing is a wicked idea." I couldn't put it better myself.

But that doesn't stop people from trying it. Advocates of market timing will argue that it's a tool to create wealth. They'll talk about the times they pulled it off, jumping out of the market just ahead of a big collapse and thereby avoiding a catastrophic hit to their portfolio. And they'll break their arms patting themselves on the back for their unmatched investing prowess.

What you'll never hear them talk about are the times they failed to recognize a disaster in the making. Nor will they cop to the fact that, while they may have managed to get out in time, they failed to get back into the market in a timely fashion, thereby missing out on huge gains. Kathy, an affluent woman in the fashion industry, is one of those people. Back in late 2008, she sold her stocks when the Dow Jones Industrial Average was around 8,500, and she was feeling pretty good about her decision as she watched it fall to as low as 6,547. Flash forward a bit more than three years, and the Dow had more than recovered its lost ground to trade at around 13,000, and Kathy was *still* sitting on the sidelines. Sure, she had saved herself from a loss of about 23 percent when she first sold, but since then, the market had recovered, stock prices had doubled from their lows, and she had missed

The Dow Jones Industrial Average, often referred to as the Dow, was created in 1896 by Charles Dow. It provides a price-weighted average of thirty of the top stocks traded on the New York Stock Exchange and the NASDAQ, including DuPont, McDonald's, the Walt Disney Company, and Nike. It is one of the most important indices in the world, and when you hear pundits talk about the "market" being up or down on any given day, they are generally referring to the Dow.

out on all those gains, including the gain of more than 40 percent from when she first sold. Why? She was paralyzed.

In order to create wealth by timing the market, one study found you had to predict correctly what the market would do next 74 percent of the time. Of course, the markets proved to be terribly uncooperative, gyrating and failing to provide analysts with any kind of discernible pattern. Little wonder the very best prognosticator the study identified ended up being able to predict what would happen next only 68.2 percent of the time. This study, by CXO Advisory Group, a Virginia firm that develops financial market models and studies market research, collected 6,582 forecasts for the S&P 500 index made by stock market gurus between 2005 and 2012, and concluded the average guru was right less than half the time. Even Jim Cramer, the host of

The main reason market timing doesn't work is because investors already know all the factors that can be known that can affect a stock's price. They are what former secretary of defense Donald Rumsfeld might have called the "known knowns." When investors receive new information about a company, they will react accordingly—buying or selling shares depending on what they've learned. Hence, all the known information is already reflected in the price of the stock. That means only surprises or shocks—Rumsfeld's "unknown unknowns"—have the potential to move markets. Because, by definition, you can't anticipate a surprise or shock, you'll never be able to time the market correctly over the long haul.

CNBC's *Mad Money*, whose fans eagerly follow his recommendations, doesn't manage a 50 percent success rate.[2]

Of course, you need to be able to make two decisions, and make them both correctly. You have to decide when to sell stocks, and then when to return to the market so you can reap the benefits of any upward climb in share value. Some individuals or pundits might get one big decision right, but both?

Again, you don't have to look much further back in time than the financial crisis of 2008 to see how this played out. Although the real drama took place that year, when the banking system came close to collapse, the stock market had begun flashing warning signals the previous summer, and that was when investors began to scurry for the exits. By the time the stock market went into freefall the following year, those who had gotten out early were bragging about their prescience, while others, panicking, rushed to sell. Now that both groups—the early movers and those who fled only after it became clear something very ugly was happening—were out of the market, they had to make a much tougher decision: when would it be safe to venture back into stocks?

Lipper is a firm that tracks how much money goes into and out of mutual funds, data that is a good barometer of what individual investors are doing. Lipper's data for these years tells us ordinary investors completely failed to profit from a stock market recovery that began in March 2009; they just weren't investing in mutual funds. By 2012 they were only just beginning to tiptoe back into mutual funds and had allowed professional investors, including institutions and others willing to tolerate the risk, to pick up the slack. Even by 2016 only about 48 percent of US households had stock market investments, according to a

Bankrate survey, down from just north of 60 percent in 2007.[3] They failed to take advantage of what will go down in history as one of the greatest buying opportunities the US stock market has ever offered. Because within about a year of the stock market hitting bottom in early 2009, the S&P 500 would rally more than 90 percent. But only a miniscule fraction of those who made the decision to get out at the right time were able, financially or psychologically, to get back *in* at the right time.

This reluctance on the part of investors to stay in the market or to recommit to stocks may have contributed to one of the most troubling socioeconomic problems confronting the United States today: the wealth gap. Numerous studies have documented that the gap between higher-income and lower-income people widened during the recovery, and that the ownership of financial assets—particularly stocks—dictated whether or not one ended up on the right side of the rift. To the extent

A mutual fund, like its name suggests, is composed of assets from many investors, each of whom "mutually" owns any securities (stocks, bonds, etc.) in which the fund manager invests the collective assets. They are great for smaller investors because they provide access to professionally managed and diversified portfolios without having to front all the assets for the fund to invest. Because the funds are mutually owned, each investor shares in any gains or losses incurred by the fund in proportion to their investment in the fund.

Americans either didn't have the ability to get back into stocks or remained too frightened to reinvest, and thus weren't able to profit from the bull market in stocks that began in March 2009, they fell further behind. Those with the resources or the intestinal fortitude to stay put and ride out the storm were able to capture the lion's share of the profits from the rally that followed.

None of this stops people from trying to dabble in market timing, of course. There are plenty of popular seasonal trading patterns that you'll probably hear about at some point, but even these are fairly suspect. For instance, the Santa Claus rally takes place around the holidays. The reasons for this rally are up for debate, but it may be the result of people investing their Christmas bonuses, tax considerations, general merriment around Wall Street, or any number of things. However, because investors have come to expect this rally, they have started trying to enter the market earlier and earlier, making it essentially a Halloween rally that will eventually turn into no rally at all.

"Sell in May and go away" is another mantra that rests on another observable trading pattern, but one that's so obscure it's hard to figure out whether there's any validity to it or just a lot of theories. The mantra means investors should dump their stocks in May and return in November, buying them at seasonal lows. Except that sometimes there are summertime rallies, and those prices aren't so low in November after all.

In fact, pretty much the only pattern you *can* count on to deliver is the one illustrated in the chart in Figure 2.1: stocks will outperform other kinds of investments over the long haul. This makes sense. When you invest in stocks, you're an owner of the company. And an owner takes on more risk than someone who lends to the company in exchange for a defined return (which is what a bond investor does). If the company goes belly-up, your investment goes with it, so in exchange for the excess risk you take on for getting in line behind bond holders in times of trouble, you receive a bigger potential upside in the form of a higher return if the company does well.

Go back and take another look at that chart at the beginning of the chapter (Figure 2.1) and you'll see how that risk/return pattern plays out in another way. Notice that the initial investment in small-cap companies paid off with three times the return as an investment in large companies. That's because smaller companies tend to be riskier investments than larger ones. These companies tend to have fewer investors because fewer investors focus on them, making them tougher to trade. They face other kinds of risks as well. For example, a small company may not be so well established, and therefore it has a higher risk of going out of business. Logically, therefore, investors will place a lower value on companies they perceive as riskier, leaving more upside to earn a higher return if things go well. And because they are smaller to start, it's easier for small companies to grow rapidly and multiply their value if they do things right. In contrast, very large companies can be subject to a version of the law of large numbers: it's harder to grow their value exponentially when their value is already so large.

At the opposite extreme, the safest investment of all is going to be cash. It's safely in the bank and the Federal Deposit Insurance Corporation will even reimburse the first $250,000 that you deposit in a US bank account if that bank goes bust. On the other hand, that money isn't generating much of a return since interest rates are currently so low; it's just sitting quietly on the sidelines earning low returns and likely losing value against inflation.

I realize not everyone likes taking risks. Some studies, for example as noted in Chapter 1, have shown women are, in fact, more risk-averse than men, especially when under stress. And there's no doubt that being in the stock market can be stressful. If you've invested the better part of your life savings in stocks only to watch the market tumble in the wake of some unfortunate economic development or headline-making global event, you might feel anxious staring at your portfolio from day to day. We'll talk in the next chapter about how your particular risk tolerance should play into your decisions about how much of your portfolio should be allocated to stocks, but even if you're inclined to sell all your shares the second they start to tip down, that's all the more reason to stay put. As I've shown, those who react rashly, whether out of fear or overconfidence in their abilities to time the market, are far more likely to lose money than those who remain invested. It should be pointed out that these quick-responders are most often men, who studies have shown tend to trade more frequently than women.[4] Yet another reason women shouldn't doubt they can be successful investors.

In the long run, you should get paid for the risk you take when you invest in stocks, and a certain amount of risk is vital to your financial well-being. But risk is like any delicacy or treat: if some is great and even necessary, and more is good, too much can do you in. After a certain point there simply isn't any way you can safely generate enough profits to justify taking that much risk.

Figuring out how much of your portfolio you want to invest in stocks is part of a process known as asset allocation, which I'll discuss in the next chapter. But before we embark on that adventure, I want to make it clear: of all the assets you could choose to include in your portfolio, stocks are the power players. Our minds may play games with us and try to trick us into doing things that are against our own best financial interests, but we can't forget that simple fact. If you have ten, twenty, or thirty years or more ahead of you, and you're trying to transform what feels like a trickle of savings into a truly impressive nest egg, your single best step is to make stocks the mainstay of your portfolio. You don't need fancy products or clever market-timing tricks. Investing just isn't that hard—contrary to all the messages sent by some Wall Street firms in attempts to preserve their own business interests. The hardest part may be resolving to just do it.

3

THE SECOND FUNDAMENTAL
Allocate Your Assets

Years ago, a friend of mine introduced me to a woman named Justine who needed some professional help making sense of her portfolio. As soon as I got a glimpse of it, I could understand why. Over the years, Justine had acquired a curious assortment of stocks, bonds, mutual funds, and other investment products, including a few index funds, shares in a bunch of technology companies, and some bonds with low credit ratings, which made them risky. And she even had some stakes in hedge funds, for which Justine was paying astronomically high fees but getting relatively little return.

When I asked Justine how she had come to own such a motley assortment of investments, she replied, somewhat sheepishly, that she had bought what she thought would do well—or in the case of the stocks and some of the mutual funds, what someone else (usually a salesman for a Wall Street firm) had told her could beat the market. (When investment professionals refer to "beating the market," they usually mean the Standard & Poor's 500 index, which means these salesmen were promising Justine that her investments would earn her a bigger return than if she'd invested in an S&P 500 index fund). In the last chapter and in the next chapter, I explain why claims of beating the market are often untrue, but the real problem with Justine's portfolio was that nobody was trying to figure out whether the oddball mix of products in it worked together as an integrated whole. In other words, nobody was evaluating her asset allocation.

The decision about how you divide your money among all the different types of investments available to you is the single most important investment decision you'll make—and it can feel like the most daunting one. Imagine being set loose in the world's biggest gourmet grocery store with no list or meal plan to guide your shopping. Instead, you meander the aisles, picking up whatever looks good. You end up with a cart full of enticing foods, but when you get home you realize you now have to make a week's worth of meals for your family and you have no idea where to start. The ingredients don't add up to anything.

Well, if you set about investing the way Justine did, picking up a little something here and something over there because it catches your eye or someone recommended it to you, the results will look like that hypothetical shopping cart: woefully inadequate to address the challenge at hand.

Instead, you need to approach the whole task from the top down. How will you divide your assets among the different asset classes available to you, from the lynchpin asset class of stocks to fixed-income products such as bonds? Within stocks, how much will you invest in large companies and those issued by smaller businesses? How much will you set aside to invest overseas? What about other factors, such as deciding how much to put to work in value stocks rather than growth stocks?

An asset class is, essentially, a grouping of investments that have similar characteristics. Stocks and bonds are large, high-level asset classes. Within each of these asset classes, you'll find sub–asset classes. For instance, the universe of stocks includes domestic stocks and international stocks. Within those asset classes, there are large company stocks and small company stocks. And then within those asset classes there are growth stocks and value stocks. In the world of bonds, you'll find bonds issued by governments and corporations, bonds issued in different currencies, as well as bonds of different lengths, or maturities, and different credit qualities.

The process of asset allocation involves figuring out what percentage of your money you should invest in each asset class. The answer depends on a variety of factors, chief among them being your age, risk tolerance, and the amount of money you have to invest. It's easiest to do this before you pick any investment products, though if you're already invested, it's never too late to take a hard look at your current allocation and figure out if it is optimal for you.

Unfortunately, many investors skip this fundamental step, choosing instead, like Justine, to rush ahead into picking out the next exciting investment opportunity. Alternatively, some simply opt to hand over their hard-earned money to an investment company in exchange for a mix of products they don't really understand and for which they will be paying lavish fees.

This really isn't surprising given that asset allocation is a comparatively unsexy process next to experimenting with investing in the latest hot investment ideas. And yet if you get it right, a well-known study has shown that the asset-allocation decision (as opposed to individual stock selections or market-timing decisions) can account for more than 90 percent of the variability of the returns in a portfolio.[1] In other words, the decisions you make about your asset allocation are more important than any other decision you make regarding how you assemble your portfolio. You're better off spending time on that than wringing your hands over which individual stocks to pick or when to get in and out of the market (which, as I explained in the last chapter, doesn't work anyway).

A few years ago, Rebecca came to me for a second opinion on whether her current portfolio made sense for her situation. She owned a mishmash of mutual funds, with holdings that seemed to overlap in many areas while leaving large gaps in others. It was the antithesis of a well-balanced portfolio—and to make matters worse, the fees on all these funds were pretty high.

It turns out Rebecca had forged a relationship with a bank to get better lending terms, and part of the deal required her to entrust a certain amount of her assets to the bank to manage. When her investment manager at the bank asked her how she wanted to invest the assets, Rebecca told him—in a move she later regretted—"Whatever makes sense." What she failed to realize was that a representative of the bank could—and likely would—interpret this to mean whatever made sense to the bank rather than what made sense to Rebecca. Instead of developing a well-thought-out asset-allocation plan for his client, and identifying inexpensive, solidly performing funds to implement the asset allocation, the bank representative instead chose funds that generated high fees for the bank. As a result, Rebecca's portfolio was filled with the bank's proprietary products, which had high fees, as well as mutual funds that generated relatively high fees for the bank. In the end, the amount of money Rebecca paid in fees to have her assets "managed" by the bank far outweighed anything she saved on the supposedly favorable lending terms, and worse yet, she had no rational asset allocation. So whether you're hiring someone to manage your funds or managing them on your own, *always* figure out your target asset allocation up front.

How to Allocate Your Assets

Your Emergency Fund

Before you figure out how to allocate the assets in your investment portfolio, you first need to figure out how much money to set aside as a safety net in case of an emergency. This money is separate from your portfolio because it is not designed for long-term savings or growth, but it is still an important step in allocating your assets.

Your emergency fund should consist of money you set aside in case of an emergency—a disability or illness that puts you out of work, loss of your job, etc.—and it should be fully funded before you start investing (with the exception that you should take advantage of 401(k) accounts that provide a "match," which I will discuss later, even if your emergency fund is not fully funded). Depending on the sources of income you have (Is your job stable? Do you have disability insurance?) you should have a sum equivalent to about six months' to a year's worth of your expenses (your rent or mortgage payments, and whatever money you need for food, clothing, health insurance payments, medication, transportation, and other incidentals) in some kind of ultrasafe vehicle, such as a bank account backed by government insurance. For some of my clients who are in, or close to, retirement, or who are anxious about investing, I have even increased this safety fund to a "living expenses" fund that includes up to three years' worth of their expenses set aside so they feel more comfortable taking risk and investing more of their portfolio in vehicles that may lose money in that three-year period.

Because there can be penalties for taking money out of investment accounts—from tax penalties for withdrawing early from a tax-sheltered retirement plan to the risk of being forced to sell stocks at a time when prices are low—your emergency fund should be in cash or a close equivalent, such as higher-yielding savings accounts or money market funds, or short-term certificates of deposits (CDs) you can access easily if necessary. Once you have set aside enough money in your emergency fund (or living expenses fund, as the case may be), you can turn your attention to making any remaining money work for you in your investment portfolio.

Asset Allocation from the Top Down

After you have your emergency fund in place, you can focus on your target asset-allocation decisions. Your core asset-allocation decision will almost always be how much to invest in the two broadest types of asset classes: stocks and fixed income (e.g., bonds and cash). In the last chapter, I explained why stocks are the best long-term investment, and as the following chart in Figure 3.1 shows, those who have bet on this asset class have been rewarded.

So why don't people just invest the majority of their money in stocks and leave it be? An entire field of behavioral finance is devoted to analyzing why people act against their own financial

Stick to Your Stocks: They'll Repay Your Loyalty

Growth of a Dollar—MSCI World Index (Net Dividends), 1970–2016

A disciplined investor looks beyond the concerns of today to the long-term growth potential of markets.

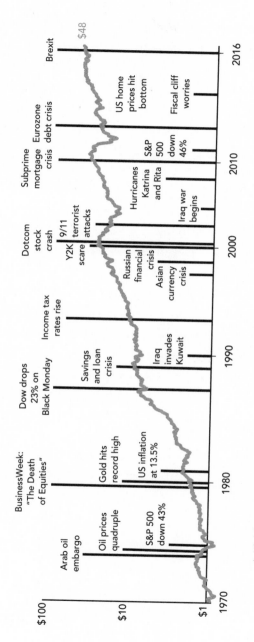

Figure 3.1

self-interest in this and other ways. Why do they insist on being distracted by glitter and market chatter instead of devoting their time to the kind of disciplined planning that would really transform their financial lives? Most often it's because they just don't have a plan in the first place. And that's why asset allocation is so important. It's a plan that imposes discipline on you, and ensures you'll stay invested during the tough times.

An asset allocation plan also ensures you don't put all your eggs in one basket and take on more risk than you are comfortable with or that is advisable depending on how long you have left before you will need to draw on the money you're investing today. My general rule of thumb is, if you won't need to use the money for at least ten years, invest it in stocks. If you're young enough— say in your twenties or thirties—you may put 90 to 100 percent of your portfolio in stocks because chances are highly likely that by the time you withdraw that money in thirty to forty years, it will have earned a much larger return than if you'd invested in fixed income. For instance, my daughter, who is in college, invests 90 percent of her small Roth IRA retirement account in stocks.

If you've been investing for a while and are closer to reaching retirement age, you likely should choose to protect some of the returns you've made and put them in relatively safe bonds and cash. The return won't be as great on these, but you can be fairly confident the money will be there when you need it, even if you happen to need it during a bear market. Later in the chapter we'll look at what your portfolio might look like as you get older and increase your assets.

Of course, when deciding your ideal asset allocation, you'll also want to consider your personal appetite for risk. You should

There are three main types of retirement accounts: 401(k)s, traditional IRAs, and Roth IRAs. A 401(k) (or a 403(b), if you work for a nonprofit) is managed by your employer, and you can only invest new money into it for as long as you work for that company. IRAs and Roth IRAs are managed by individuals, which gives you greater autonomy to choose your investments and align them with your asset-allocation plan. For traditional IRAs and 401(k)s you don't pay taxes on any assets you deposit in them but are taxed when you withdraw the funds in retirement (or before). Roth IRAs, on the other hand, are taxed up front but not when you withdraw the funds. These can be great for young people who are just starting out and in a relatively low tax bracket because they can invest income essentially tax-free (because their tax liability will be low now and they won't have to pay taxes later on withdrawals from the Roth IRA) and grow it over a long time.

never take on more risk than you can tolerate, because you don't want to end up so anxious about what's happening to your investments that you can't sleep or—worse yet—that you fall into a panic when the market is down and decide to sell those riskier and better long-term performers just in order to sleep. This is a very real thing that I have seen with some of my clients—they'll come to me and say they want an aggressive portfolio full of stocks and short on fixed-income investments, but when the market starts to dip, they call me in a panic and wonder if they should move some of their money around. This is why a good

asset-allocation plan is so important; if done right at the beginning, it can provide stress relief, enabling you to ride out the
market downturns knowing you have a longer-term plan to grow
your assets, and that riding out the downturns is part of the plan.

Asset Allocation: Risk & Reward

Annualized Return (%) 1973–2013 and its Effect
on the Growth of $10,000* (One-Year Return)

% STOCKS/ FIXED INCOME	RETURN	LOWEST	HIGHEST	END WEALTH
100/0	13.8%	-51.0%	82.25%	$2.00 million
80/20	12.6%	-42.4%	63.2%	$1.27 million
60/40	11.2%	-32.6%	45.8%	$768,383
0/100	6.6%	0.3%	22.6%	$127,351

The stock-bond decision drives a large part of your portfolio's long-term performance.

*Asset allocation based on Dimensional Fund Advisor Balanced Index Strategies:
Summary Statistics, December 31, 2013. Past performance is no guarantee of future
results. Use is for illustrative purposes only: based on the performance of indexes
with model/back-tested asset allocations and does not include fees or expenses. Data
sources: S&P 500 Index and Dow Jones US Select REIT Index: data © S&P Dow Jones
Indices, its affiliates and/or licensors. All rights reserved; FTSE Russell Indices: Russell
data copyright Frank Russell Company 1995–2016, all rights reserved; MSCI data ©
MSCI 2017, all rights reserved; Fama/French Indices source Ken French website with
permission, all rights reserved; Bloomberg Barclays US Treasury 1–5 Yr. Total Return
Index–Ticker: LTR1TRUU data Source: Bloomberg Index Services Limited, all rights
reserved; Citigroup World Government Bond Index © 2016 Citigroup Index LLC All rights
reserved; BofA Merrill Lynch One-Year US Treasury Note Index: Source BofA Merrill
Lynch Global Research, used with permission.

But even if you have an aversion to risk, you still have to take on enough to meet your goals. Risk and return are correlated: the more risk you take, the greater your chance for a return—and a loss. As you can see from the preceding chart, the way you construct your asset allocation can lead to very different investment outcomes. One individual investor putting $10,000 to work in 1973 could have ended up with anywhere from $127,351 to $2 million by the time she retired forty years later! And the only thing that explains that difference? How that woman divided up her assets between stocks and bonds.

Let's take a closer look at some of the data. During the forty-year period shown in the chart, if you had 60 percent of your portfolio invested in stocks and 40 percent in fixed income, the worst-performing twelve-month period your portfolio would have experienced (during the financial crisis of 2008) would have resulted in a loss of 32.6 percent. The bonds in the portfolio would have served as a nice cushion, helping to soften the hard landing as the stocks crashed. Of course, there would have been a trade-off, as the best performance during any twelve-month period would have been only 45.8 percent (this period, by the way, began in 2009, immediately after the worst twelve months). That's a far cry from the more than 80 percent someone who had kept all their investments in stocks would have enjoyed; this time around, the lower returns from bonds dampened the gains the stock market posted during a massive rally.

That's a reasonable trade-off, especially because an 80 percent gain isn't enough to recover a 51 percent loss. (If you lose 50 percent, you have to make 100 percent to get back to your starting point. For example, if you start out with $100 and lose half of that, you are left with $50, which has to double, or increase

100 percent in value, to get back to your original starting point.)

But what happens if you stay that conservative—maintaining a 60/40 split between stocks and bonds over the long term? The chart shows you the answer. For the sake of comparison, let's assume you had invested 100 percent of your $10,000 into stocks and stuck to your guns over the next forty years. You would have generated an average annual return of 13.8 percent, yielding $2 million after riding out all the stock market's boom-and-bust cycles. But if you had opted to put $6,000 into stocks and $4,000 into bonds, your returns would look very different.

On the surface, the average annual return for the more conservative asset allocation doesn't appear to be *that* much lower than for 100 percent stocks: 11.2 percent, or a mere 2.6 percentage points lower. Except over the course of forty years, that difference adds up, or more accurately, that difference compounds. Each year you missed out on those 2.6 percentage points' worth of returns, you lost the opportunity to reinvest those returns into higher-earning stocks. (As we'll show in chapter 6, the same thing would happen if you paid 2.6 percent in fees, because you also can't reinvest into the market the money you spend on fees.) How much of a difference does that make? Well, as you can see, the 60 percent stock portfolio would leave you with a $768,383 portfolio after forty years—more than $1.2 million less than if you'd invested 100 percent in stocks.

If you take a look at the preceding detailed chart, you can see just how much apparently small variations in average annual returns can affect what you end up with at the end of your investment period. An 80/20 split in favor of stocks would have produced an average annual return of 12.6 percent, a maximum one-year loss of 42.4 percent and a maximum one-year gain of

63.2 percent—and your $10,000 investment would have turned into $1.27 million over that forty-year period. And as the chart shows, while investing 100 percent of your portfolio into bonds from 1973 to 2013 would certainly have been better than shoving your money under the mattress and hoping the house didn't burn down, it would have yielded only 6.6% on average each year, ending with $127,351—a nice sum of money, to be sure, but not nearly enough for you to retire comfortably.

Going forward, the all-bond option is likely going to be even less appealing. Not only do bonds currently offer even less return than before, but they possess more risk than usual, because we're in the last stages of a rally in bonds that lasted more than three decades. As investors have flocked to bonds in search of safety and some kind of income, bond prices have soared, driving their yields—the interest rate paid to investors—lower. Now, with the Federal Reserve (the Fed)—the central bank of the United States—likely to continue raising interest rates, it's reasonable to expect downward pressure on bond prices. We're still in the early stages of what is likely going to be a years-long transformation that could well end up making bonds riskier to own than stocks. As interest rates rise, existing bonds (which carry lower rates) become less valuable to potential investors because they will end up yielding a lower return than any bonds purchased under the newer, higher interest rate. The prices of existing bonds can be expected to decrease as interest rates rise.

For example, let's say you own a $10,000 bond that pays an annual interest rate of 2 percent, giving you an annual interest income of $200. If interest rates double to 4 percent, someone can buy a newly issued $10,000 bond and collect an annual income of $400 for their $10,000, rather than the $200 annual

Bond prices and interest rates move in opposite directions. As interest rates rise, existing bonds will see their prices fall, because their interest payments to investors are based on older, lower interest rates. As the bonds' prices fall, the yield to maturity will rise until it reaches an equilibrium with the higher interest rate at which new bonds are now being priced and sold to investors. This repricing mechanism makes old, existing bonds competitive with those that will be newly issued to investors.

income you got. To make your bond an attractive option in the market, a potential buyer would insist that its price to be cut so that it competes with the newly-issued bonds. As its price declines, its yield to maturity would rise to the point where it is in line with current interest rates. (Yield to maturity is the annual total return expected on a bond if the bond is held until its end date.) In this specific example, the price would have to fall enough that the $200 annual interest payment, plus increases in the value of the bond as its maturity date approaches, would translate to an annual payment of about 4 percent. Your bond is just no longer as valuable as it used to be. So if you own bonds in a rising-interest-rate environment, inevitably you are going to suffer as you watch their prices fall, and you will collect relatively meager streams of income: an unenviable state of affairs.

Because the Fed has set interest rates so low for the past few years in order to encourage borrowing, it's reasonable to expect that we'll see long-term downward pressure on bond prices over the next few years as the government raises interest rates to be more in line with the current state of the economy and to try to get back to more normal interest rates. This means that even the relatively unimpressive returns of bonds (compared to the returns of stocks) seen over the past several decades might not be able to be achieved by someone entering the bond market today. And the longer the time horizon of the bond, the more it is at risk of going down when interest rates rise.

That doesn't mean, though, that you should just invest all your money in stocks. Everyone has a different tolerance for risk,

The correlation between a bond's time horizon and the risk that its value will go down as interest rates rise can be explained by a rule of thumb related to the bond's **duration**. The duration of a bond is a measurement of how quickly you will receive the money you expect to receive from the bond (e.g., a combination of the bond's maturity date and its coupon or interest payments). For example, a bond that matures in ten years might have a duration of about eight years because you will be receiving coupon payments during the ten years, and then the principal back at the end of the ten years. Interest rates and duration have an inverse correlation, with the following rule of thumb: **when interest rates go up, the value of a bond generally goes down by the duration of the bond multiplied by the percent by which interest rates rose.** So for example, that ten-year bond with an eight-year duration would lose 8 percent if interest rates rose 1 percent, or would lose 16 percent if interest rates rose 2 percent (i.e., 8 x 2% = 16%). So when interest rates are rising, bonds are especially risky. And the longer the bond's duration, the more risky it will be because the more it will be exposed to interest rate risk.

and it's imperative to figure out what yours is when determining your asset allocation. If you're going to lose sleep whenever the stock market falls or when the pundits on TV are shouting at you to sell, you should opt to allocate some investments to safer, less risky investment vehicles such as cash and relatively short duration bonds in order to preserve your sanity.

What you ultimately decide to do is up to you, but before you figure out how risk-tolerant or -averse you are, you first need to understand exactly what "risk" means. Many of us think of risk simply as volatility, and the folks on TV encourage us in that belief. They gasp when the market soars and dips and shout all sorts of conflicting messages that keep us awake at night.

Volatility, by its nature, is scary because we can't control it, nor can we get rid of it. Plus it reminds us of what can happen if the market roller coaster gets stuck at the bottom of a nasty dip and we, in turn, are left with big negative numbers on our financial statements.

Not all volatility is bad, however. True, some turbulent days in the markets can be horrifying, leaving us feeling as if we've been on a roller coaster, but we can still end the day with our portfolios in precisely the same place they were when markets opened that morning; we haven't lost a penny because the market bounced back. Volatility also describes what happens when the stock market soars, generating large gains. In these cases, you can end the day with a broad grin on your face and a nice profit. In general, the thing to keep in mind during volatile times is that you are getting paid for taking on this volatility because risk and return correlate. That is why your high-level decision about what percentage of your portfolio to invest in stocks is so important.

Secondary, but Still Essential, Asset-Allocation Decisions: Further Diversification

Once you decide how much of your portfolio will go into equities (stocks) versus fixed income (bonds and cash), you'll need to decide how to diversify your portfolio further by breaking each of these primary categories down among narrower sub-asset classes. For instance, within the vast universe of stocks, you can choose to put money into US and international stocks, into stocks of large and small companies, and into growth and value companies. All of these will have different patterns of returns, and how you divide your assets among these options will result in very different investment outcomes. The same is true of bonds, where even if you choose to invest only in government bonds, you can still opt for short-term bonds (usually less risky but with lower interest rates) or longer-term bonds. You may even decide you want to own bonds issued by a foreign government and by corporations with various credit ratings; the higher the credit rating, the lower the risk and usually the lower the potential return.

Let's say you decide to put 80 percent of your money into stocks. Why not just put 100 percent of your stock allocation into the S&P 500 index and forget about it? After all, this index represents the biggest companies out there, and there are plenty of cheap and accessible investment products you can use to buy the S&P 500. With one simple, fast decision, you could own a stake in about 80 percent of the entire US stock market, by value. But the United States stock market only accounts for the value of about half the world's stock markets so you'd still be turning your back on a lot of other options. Plus, what about the 20 to 25 percent of the US market the S&P 500 doesn't cover? There is more value to be found there.

When you dig into the world of stocks, you'll find that what happens to the S&P 500 doesn't tell the full story of what is afoot with stocks as a group. Nor does it represent the vast majority of American companies with stocks available for purchase. As its name suggests, the S&P 500 includes stocks for the top 500 publicly traded companies in the United States, but the remaining 20 or 25 percent of US market value includes stocks belonging to thousands of smaller companies in the mid-cap and small-cap size categories, whose returns are often very different from their larger counterparts at different times. That's just what happened during what has become known as "the lost decade" for investors, the period between 2001 to the end of 2011. During these years, the S&P 500 took investors on a wild ride but rewarded them a paltry average annual return of just 2.93 percent, just slightly beating inflation, with those returns coming mostly from dividends paid out by the companies in the index rather than from the increase in the value of the companies in the index (capital gains). The value of the stocks that made up the S&P 500 index itself did not increase much at all.

But while those big stocks were disappointing investors, smaller stocks were stealthily, in the background, doing much better (in relative terms), and many fared spectacularly well in absolute terms. In fact, during the same lost decade, buying a DFA asset class fund of small stocks, those that represented about 10 percent of the total market value in the US stock markets, would have earned you an average annual return of 6.8 percent—more than double that of the S&P 500. (DFA stands for Dimensional Fund Advisors, a company that has many different asset class index funds, as shown on the chart.)

When you become a small-stock investor, you end up taking

on more risk because these companies are smaller. Their shares also don't usually trade as frequently, which means if you decide to unload your positions, it may end up proving difficult to sell lots of stock quickly without losing some money for the privilege of selling when you want. These companies have a market capitalization (the stock price multiplied by the number of company shares issued) of less than about $2 billion each, compared to $5 billion or more for large-cap companies. By way of comparison, Apple, one of the market's largest publicly traded companies, has (at the time of this writing) a valuation of about $700 billion.

But among the smaller companies, you'll probably find many names you know or have heard of. Children's clothing retailer Children's Place is a small-cap company, as is Forrester Research. Domino's Pizza was, until it "graduated" to the ranks of a middle-size company ("mid-cap"), while larger companies acquired other small-cap firms such as Peet's Coffee & Tea and Harry Winston jewelers. There is also an asset category of even smaller stocks—so-called micro-cap companies—with a market capitalization of about $300 million or less, which includes businesses such as Elizabeth Arden and Rosetta Stone. Again demonstrating the truth of the adage that higher risk translates into higher rewards, micro-cap companies fared even better than small-cap ones during the lost decade, with the DFA Micro Cap asset class fund posting average annual gains of 6.9 percent.

In the same way that you don't want a portfolio that is full of only stocks or only bonds, you also want to invest in a range of stocks with different characteristics, including size, which we discussed earlier, but also whether they're foreign or domestic, growth or value. And if you combine size and value characteristics, that can be even more powerful in diversifying

The "Lost Decade" That Wasn't . . . If You Diversified

Annual Investment Returns—
10 Years Ending December 31, 2011

US Large Companies (S&P 500)	2.93%
DFA US Large Cap Value (DFLVX)	4.5%
DFA US Small Cap (DFSTX)	6.8%
DFA US Small Cap Value (DFSVX)	7.9%
DFA US Micro Cap (DFSCX)	6.9%
DFA US Real Estate (DFREX)	10.1%
DFA International Large Cap Value (DFIVX)	7.8%
DFA International Small Cap (DFISX)	11.2%
DFA International Small Value (DISVX)	12.0%
DFA Emerging (DFEMX)	13.6%
DFA Emerging Value (DFEVX)	16.8%
DFA Emerging Small Cap (DEMSX)	16.2%
US government fixed income	6.39%

your portfolio, as the preceding chart shows. While small-cap stocks earned an average annual return of 6.8 percent during the lost decade, investing in the DFA small-cap *value* funds earned 7.9 percent on average per year. Adding a *third* diversifying characteristic, and choosing to invest in the DFA international small-value funds, generated average returns of 12 percent—nearly double that of plain US small stocks, and quadruple that of the S&P 500.

In the long run, as we've discussed already, small company stocks have had better returns than large company stocks. The same is true of value stocks compared to growth stocks. Value stocks are stocks that are out of favor or relatively unpopular, which makes their book value relatively low. Book value is the value of the company's assets as they appear on its balance sheet. Think of it as what would be left in value if the company went out of business today. For value companies, the price of its stock divided by its per-share book value is relatively low, maybe less than 1.5 or even around 1 (for comparison, the S&P 500 average book value was about 2.4 in the summer of 2016). Another shorthand way to think of a company's value is its price-to-earnings ratio, or its P/E. This is the number you get when you divide the price of a stock by its annual earnings per share. A value stock traditionally trades at a price that is only ten to fifteen times (or less) its annual profits, whereas its growth counterpart could trade at twenty, thirty, forty, or many more times its earnings. (I've seen growth stocks trade at hundreds of times earnings, and some where this price-to-earnings ratio—a key barometer of valuation—becomes completely irrelevant, such as with the dot-com stocks, whose lack of earnings made their price-to-earnings ratio an infinitely large number.)

Value Stocks vs. Growth Stocks

Growth stocks, as their name suggests, tend to belong to companies whose earnings and/or revenues are expected to grow rapidly; as a result, their stock price may also increase quickly and carry a valuation premium awarded by investors who don't mind paying a higher price in exchange for the expected high growth rate. Value stocks, on the other hand, may be slower growing but are appealing because their valuations are lower than the market average, and they may pay relatively high dividends to their shareholders. They are like buying something at a discounted price because the demand for them is not as high as for the hot growth stocks. In the long run, value stocks have had higher returns than growth stocks—it's easier to beat low expectations. The famous investor Warren Buffett favors value stocks. This is only one of the possible ways in which investors can segment the stock universe into different asset categories—and determining how much you should invest in growth and value stocks is just one of the decisions to make in deciding your asset allocation.

In contrast to growth stocks such as the dot-com stocks, value stocks aren't glamorous, or the kinds of stocks you want to brag about at dinner parties. As their name implies, value stocks can offer a good deal to those able to ignore the hype around the hottest, most in-demand stocks and dig beneath the surface to find stocks that might be priced below what they're worth. For example, if you were investing in 2001, you probably would have wanted to own shares in Motorola, a company poised to take advantage of the explosive growth in mobile phones. Meanwhile, you might have ignored Hormel Foods, a 100-plus-year-old company that manufactures SPAM and Dinty Moore beef stew, among many other grocery store staples. But over the following decade, during which mobile phones became a "must-own" device, Motorola shares lost more than 50 percent of their value. In contrast, shares of Hormel Foods boomed, soaring 185 percent. More often than not, value stocks that seem boring end up delivering better returns than do the high-flying growth stocks because they have a better chance to beat the relatively low expectations the market has set for them. That's why I ensure my clients have more exposure to value stocks than to growth stocks as part of their asset allocation (i.e., I "overweight" value stocks), and why I'd recommend you do the same.

Adding some international flavor can also diversify your portfolio, because there are times that international stocks do better than US stocks. That certainly was the case during the lost decade, when international markets outperformed those in the United States. Even investing in large value companies in Europe and Japan and other developed countries through a DFA asset class fund would have produced an average annual return of 7.8 percent—more than twice that of the S&P 500. As we can see in the preceding chart, international small-value companies did exceptionally well, with the DFA fund for that asset class earning an average of 12 percent per year. But for emerging markets— places such as India, China, or Brazil that are experiencing periods of transition toward a developed, capitalist market and are therefore prone to turbulence—these were great years. Because the rate of growth in emerging markets was so much higher than in more established economies, they posted average annual returns for value stocks and small-cap stocks that topped 16 percent. An investor who had put $1,000 into those DFA emerging market asset class funds in 2001 would have ended up with more than $4,000 by 2011; someone who had invested it in the S&P 500 during that same period would have ended up with only $1,335.

Of course, you never know in advance what's going to do well and what will do poorly, which is why you want a blend of all these asset classes. You want a well-structured and diversified asset-allocation plan for much the same reason you want a healthy, well-balanced diet. Too much (or too little) of any one food group throws your system out of whack and threatens your well-being; the same is true for asset classes.

The period that has followed the lost decade has illustrated the downside of taking on too much risk in pursuit of returns by concentrating your investments in a risky asset that did well recently. Anyone who sat down in 2012 and studied the patterns represented by the preceding chart may have been tempted to put a lot of her portfolio in emerging markets small stocks. But she would soon have regretted it because emerging markets fared much worse than other asset classes in the five years after 2011. In 2015, some emerging market asset class funds fell by as much as 17 percent. A handful of stocks in these markets might ride out the storm, but by and large all suffered simply because they are part of a category that is being swept by large and powerful economic forces.

In the same time emerging markets began to suffer, the S&P stocks regained traction, taking over as market leaders, turning in outsize returns and leaving the smaller stocks to languish in their shadow (until 2016, when small-company stocks came into favor again). And while in the long run value stocks have outperformed growth stocks, growth stocks dominated the market from after the lost decade until 2015, just as they did during the dot-com boom. (In their most recent incarnation, everybody wanted to talk about the FANG stocks—Facebook, Amazon, Netflix, and Google.) By mid-February 2017 the roller coaster took another jolt upward, and suddenly emerging markets were once again a best-performing global asset class. By the time you read this, who knows?

You can't plan for surprises like these, so you want to be prepared for all of them—both good and bad—by spreading out your exposure as much as possible and reducing your risk that any one of these inevitable surprises will have an outsize effect on your portfolio.

When I'm helping my clients develop their own asset-allocation plans, my first step is to look at stocks because, as the First Fundamental spells out, they are the asset class that should offer the best long-term returns. For those of my clients who are living in the United States and plan to retire here, I want to design an asset allocation that is "overweight" US stocks—typically more than 60 percent of the stock portion of the portfolio. This is for two reasons: They'll be retiring in the US, so it makes sense for their assets to be invested here. And the US market is relatively business-friendly, transparent, and ruled by law. (In contrast, in a country such as China, you may invest in businesses that are profitable, but as an individual foreign investor, you may never benefit from those profits as much as you should because their markets are generally not as transparent or protective of investors as the US legal system is of investors in the US markets.)

How you determine your own weightings among subclasses is ultimately up to you, but if you're looking for guidance, follow the same rule of thumb I proposed earlier in the chapter—the older you get, the more it makes sense to set aside a larger portion of your money in safe, fixed-income vehicles. But this should also depend on your appetite for risk. Also consider that even if you are on the verge of retirement and are relatively risk-averse, it still makes sense for you to keep a significant portion of your money in the relatively risky but potentially higher-returning asset classes because you likely will still need your investments working for you while you are in retirement. And for women who have more in assets than they will need for their retirement, you may want to focus a portion of your assets on investing for the next generations or for eventual charitable giving. In that case, keeping a large portion of those assets in the stock markets will likely make sense.

What About Other Types of Stock Asset Classes, Such as Real Estate, Commodities, and Hedge Funds?

People always ask me if they should add real estate products to their investment portfolio if they already own real estate by owning a home or some other type of real estate property. I believe you should, because real estate as an additional stock asset class will provide further diversification for your portfolio. The real estate asset class should include both residential and commercial real estate, and both domestic and international real estate. So while you may own the home you live in, it is an illiquid asset that hopefully will increase in value over time. But that is a different investment than a broadly diversified fund of real estate assets that should provide an income stream from any rent the properties receive, as well as provide returns from their increase in value over time, with different real estate markets doing well at different times.

In contrast to real estate, which should produce income for

you, I do not believe it's worth it to put a significant portion of your investments in the asset class that tracks commodities. The best way I can explain my reasoning is to ask you the same question that Warren Buffett asked in his 2011 letter to shareholders: Which would you rather own, all the gold in the world (which, if you shaped it into a cube, would fit into the center of a baseball infield) or all the cropland in the United States, plus sixteen corporations the size of ExxonMobil? At the time Buffett asked this question, both had the same market value: $9.6 trillion. But to Buffett the real value of the latter was much greater, because it was—and is—a group of productive assets. Gold, meanwhile, can't be used to produce anything of value; its price simply rises and falls based on what someone else is willing to pay for it. To borrow Buffett's view of gold, it's the ultimate lazy asset. He'd rather own an asset that can produce some kind of return, whether it's a dividend or even crops. So if I add gold or any other commodities, such as oil and agricultural goods, to my clients' portfolios, I make a point of keeping the percentage in their asset allocation very small, and I treat it mostly as an inflation hedge because commodities usually go up in value with inflation. But even as an inflation hedge, commodities don't always work because their price doesn't always correlate with inflation.

Regarding hedge funds, I do not consider them a separate asset class worth owning for two main reasons. First, they are really not a separate asset class. Hedge funds are one of the most alluring products offered to individual investors as a way for them to "build wealth." Unfortunately, the vast majority of them do no such thing. And their name is a misnomer because many hedge funds do not hedge at all. While the complicated arguments they use to market themselves are very seductive, they don't fit into a sensible asset-allocation plan because you often have no idea what they will be invested in at any time.

What most hedge funds have in common is not that they hedge but that they have eye-poppingly high fees that get even higher when you earn a return: a typical hedge fund charges a 2 percent management fee (compared to as little as 0.25 percent (or even less) for an index fund) and on top of that its managers usually charge 20 percent of any profits the investments make. Plus, unlike mutual funds, there's no efficient public market to trade in most hedge funds, so once you buy into one, it may be difficult to extricate yourself from it. Moreover, in addition to being hard to use in developing an asset-allocation plan, hedge funds fail the next three rules too: they certainly aren't index funds because they do a lot of "active management"; they can make it difficult to rebalance your portfolio because you likely won't know what they are invested in; and their fees are astronomical. (More about these three problems with hedge funds later.)

Once you've decided on the asset class weighting within your stock asset allocation, you can do the same thing for the fixed-income side, for your bonds and cash. In general, I view the fixed-income side as the portfolio's safety ballast, helping me to balance and diversify the risk I'm taking in the stock portion. So I usually limit the bond side to fairly conservative fixed-income investments such as relatively short-term, high-quality corporate and government bonds, and even money market funds. A money market fund aims to earn interest for its investors while not losing money. To keep the investments that safe, money market funds invest in very short-term, high-quality, liquid fixed-income investments. They are low-cost, low-risk, and therefore earn relatively low returns.

Asset Allocation Decision

Flow Chart

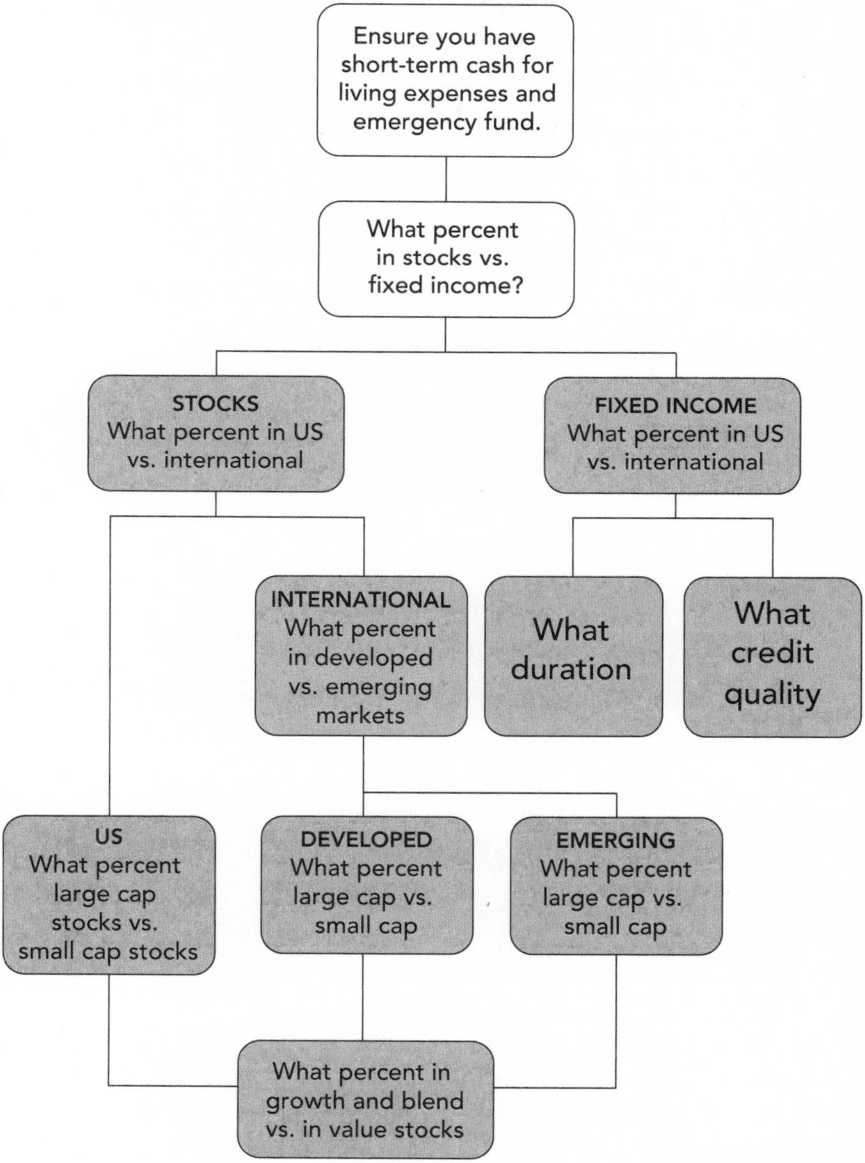

Figure 3.2

Wondering what your asset allocation might look like? If you are just starting out investing in a 401(k) account or some type of IRA account, and you have a decades-long time horizon, I suggest you keep it simple to start and invest in two funds: invest about two-thirds in a broadly diversified US stock index fund, and the rest in a broadly diversified international stock index fund. If it's more money than you feel comfortable investing all in stocks, carve out a certain portion to keep in a conservative short-term bond fund or in a money market fund.

If you're in your twenties or thirties and have somewhere between $10,000 and $50,000 to invest, you might put 80 percent of your money into stocks and 20 percent into bonds, with the stock portion overweighting the US but still including a significant exposure to international stocks. The portfolio might look something like this:

STOCK ASSET CLASSES	PERCENT
US stocks including large and small	52%
Developed International (large and small)	28%
Total Stocks	80%
Fixed income asset classes	
High-quality relatively short-term bonds	15%
Cash or cash equivalents (e.g., money market funds)	5%

Alternatively, an investor in her 40s or 50s, with savings of $100,000 to $250,000 to put to work, might have an ideal asset allocation that is slightly more skewed in favor of bonds because she is older and may want to start dialing back her amount of risk. So, a mix of 70 percent stocks and 30 percent fixed income might be appropriate. Again, I'd ensure that the asset allocation overweighted value stocks and emphasized the United States but still included a significant portion invested internationally. Her portfolio might look something like this:

STOCK ASSET CLASSES	PERCENT
US stocks including large and small	39%
US Large Cap Value	6%
Developed International (large and small)	11%
Developed International Value	4%
Emerging Market Stocks	7%
Global Real estate	3%
Total Stocks	70%
Fixed income asset classes	
High-quality relatively short-term bonds	25%
Cash or cash equivalents (e.g., money market funds)	5%

If you're in your forties or fifties and have more than $500,000 on hand, I'd suggest the same basic 70/30 mix of stock and bonds. However, because you have more assets to invest, you can afford to take some additional smaller positions. I don't encourage you to do this unless you have a significant amount of money to invest, because the more positions you have, the more you have to pay in fees to manage them. For example, if you have $10,000 to invest and put 3 percent in emerging markets small company stocks, that would be only $300. Just to purchase a position in that may cost you more than 2 percent of the $300, which is a relatively high price to pay for such a small position. But if you're investing 3 percent of $500,000, you'll have $15,000 to allocate to that asset class, making it much more affordable to take this position. With that in mind, your portfolio might resemble the chart on page 93.

Once you are close to retirement, you likely will want a more conservative portfolio, such as a 60 percent stock/40 percent fixed-income asset allocation. Or even 50/50 depending on your situation and risk tolerance. But remember again, you do need your money to continue to grow so you can have the resources you need for the rest of your life. And if you already have those resources, it may make sense to be more aggressive with some of the assets because you might at that point be investing the assets for your heirs and/or charities you want to support.

The larger your portfolio grows, the more you might find it's worth your while to consult with a financial adviser about your asset-allocation targets. Whether you decide to work with a financial adviser or manage your portfolio on your own, I hope you now understand why the asset-allocation decision is so critical. Get it right, and it lays a solid foundation. Get it wrong, and

STOCK ASSET CLASSES	PERCENT
US large company (e.g., S&P 500)	32%
US large-cap value	6%
US small-cap value	4%
US micro cap	3%
Developed international	8%
Developed international value	4%
Developed international small value	3%
Emerging market value	4%
Emerging market small company	3%
Global real estate	3%
Total Stocks	70%
Fixed income asset classes	
High-quality relatively short-term bonds	25%
Cash or cash equivalents (e.g., money market funds)	5%

even doing other things right (such as keeping a firm eye on your costs) won't benefit you as much as they could have. Asset allocation *matters*. Big time.

How Often Should I Change My Asset Allocation?

Can you tweak your asset allocation as the mood strikes you, or should you set it and forget it? As I said previously, you'll likely want to reallocate your assets as you get older in order to reduce your risk. But what if you're tempted to make changes in the short term? From time to time, you'll probably hear people talking (or arguing) about why something (such as gold, other commodities, or hedge funds) is (or isn't) an asset class, and why it does (or doesn't) deserve a place in your asset-allocation model. Regarding what is an asset class that you should include in your portfolio, that decision should not change, assuming you've made informed decisions to start.

Regarding your secondary asset-allocation decisions (such as how much you invest in large or small companies as a percentage of your overall stock allocation), those shouldn't change often at all either. Unless the underlying assumptions on which you based your decisions change, there's no reason to start messing around with anything. For individual investors who are just starting out and managing their own portfolios using broad index funds that cover the whole world (which I will discuss in the next chapter), you probably won't need to make changes to your secondary asset allocation because the funds themselves will do the adjusting for you as the world changes. Even when I have very affluent clients with large portfolios, I'm very conservative when it comes to changing their asset allocation. Sure, they may have a detailed asset-allocation target, with many sub-asset classes, but I won't add new ones or alter weightings unless I learn something that changes my view of those asset classes significantly, convincing me their performance will change dramatically over the long run.

That doesn't happen very often. Still, several years ago I remember learning about the ways fracking technologies were transforming the energy industry and how fracking ultimately would make the United States energy-independent. This would be a tremendous boost for the US economy and would deliver a shock to oil and gas companies, which would have to rethink their supply-and-demand economics as fracking sent supplies soaring. Knowing this, I cut my clients' (already small) target exposure to commodities such as oil and increased their exposure to US stocks, which should benefit from a stronger economy. But events like this are pretty rare. Only infrequently can I identify a situation where something is so transformative that it really makes sense for me to recommend a change in the target asset allocation. Normally, changing your asset allocation in response to every world event would be too much like trying to time the market. As I have already shown you, that is usually a game for losers.

Now that you've decided which asset classes to own and in what percentages, how do you go about buying them? That leads us to the Third Fundamental.

4

THE THIRD
FUNDAMENTAL
Implement Using
Index Funds

Back in 1951, a Princeton undergrad by the name of Jack Bogle decided to undertake a study of the mutual fund industry for his undergraduate thesis project. At the time, he was simply curious about the stock market, but what he learned would eventually lead to a revolution in the way individual investors—like you—could make the most of their money.

A mutual fund is an investment vehicle composed of stocks or bonds from a wide range of companies and is, as its name suggests, "mutually" owned by all the investors in the fund. The traditional mutual fund is what is known as an "actively managed" fund, meaning the fund managers pick individual stocks for their investors based on how they think each of them will fare.

But back in 1951, Bogle encountered the problem that decades later, at Vanguard, he would set out to solve: the mutual fund managers of the 1950s did a bad job of producing returns. Seventy-five percent of the managers Bogle studied failed to outperform the average of all the stocks in the market, especially after taking into account the costs of running the funds and the taxes investors had to pay on the profits they did earn.

Bogle wasn't alone in pointing out that this conventional mutual fund structure did investors a disservice. Academics such as Burton Malkiel, Eugene Fama, and Paul French all conducted hard research into why this was happening, and in 1973 Malkiel shared his findings in what would become the classic book *A Random Walk Down Wall Street*. "What we need," Malkiel wrote, "is a no-load, minimum management-fee mutual fund that simply buys the hundreds of stocks making up the broad stock market averages and does no trading from security to security in an attempt to catch the winners."

Clearly, Bogle was paying attention because, just one year later, he set up the mutual fund company Vanguard Group. Bogle's mission was to resolve the inefficiency that existed with actively managed funds by identifying a basket of stocks he believed replicated the market and then building an investment product that would allow investors to own all the stocks in that basket. This investment product was known as an "index fund" because it was composed of stocks of companies in a particular market index (an index, such as the Standard & Poor's 500 or Dow Jones Industrial Average, measures the value of a particular segment of the market). If Bogle picked an index that was big enough, such as the S&P 500 index, he could give investors access to 75 or 80 percent of the value of all the publicly traded companies in the United States.

So that's precisely what he did. Thus was born the Standard

& Poor's 500-stock fund: the first mutual fund tied to the performance of a stock market index that was available to ordinary investors. One of its best features—in addition to the fact that with a single investment decision, an investor could end

An index fund is a mutual fund (managed by a mutual fund company) or an exchange-traded fund designed to track a particular market index. You'll see the latter called by its acronym, an ETF, but it's basically an index product that trades on a stock exchange, unlike a mutual fund, which you can only buy from and sell to the mutual fund company at the end of the day.

Index funds provide diversification alongside a low cost structure. The most popular and best-known of these are designed to track the S&P 500 index, one of the biggest and most actively traded stock market indices in the world. But there are many, many other indexes, some of them very well-known, and others that have been custom-designed by index providers or banks precisely so they can then create an index fund around them. There are US small company value index funds and emerging markets index funds—and green energy index funds. Regardless of what part of the world or market theme you want to track, you'll probably find an index fund to help you do it more cheaply than actively managed funds, and with a guaranteed amount of diversification. Best of all, an index fund probably will outperform active managers investing in the same asset class, especially on an after-fee and after-tax basis.

up owning such a diverse portfolio—was the fact that the fees were so low, because Vanguard didn't have to pay the research expenses other mutual fund firms did in order to pick the stocks in the fund. Nonetheless, rivals initially scoffed at Vanguard as Bogle's Folly, and in its initial year, the world's first retail index fund attracted only $11 million from wary investors.

But time has proven that Bogle made the right call, and Vanguard has become the granddaddy of an entire industry, spawning scores of other index fund products. From that initial $11 million in assets, the company has grown to manage $4 trillion of investors' money across 170 countries. The result is a boon for investors like myself and my clients, who believe using index funds provides the best chance for you to have a portfolio that performs well and generates wealth over the long haul.

Despite all these seemingly obvious upsides, most investors still seem to prefer actively managed mutual funds to index funds. Morningstar, the Chicago-based firm that tracks mutual fund data, calculates that more than four decades after Vanguard launched its world-changing index fund, investors have a mere 23 percent of all US mutual fund assets in index funds.[1] And that doesn't include all the money people invest in individual stocks, hoping to outperform the market.

This data tells me that a lot of investors are walking away from a big opportunity and instead investing in products that, at the very least, won't help them build wealth as efficiently as they could. Over and over again, I find myself talking to people who use actively managed funds, probably because they seem so much more exciting than index funds, and/or because someone sold them these actively managed funds. Instead of following a model, these active funds are overseen by a real, live manager who can talk on TV about his stock picks and tell stories about how he "discovered" the hidden value that existed there or about the dramatic turnaround under way in a previously struggling manufacturing company. These stories grab your attention, and it is, without a doubt, impressive to hear someone speak so articulately about a world that can seem so murky and unpredictable to outsiders. What could possibly go wrong?

Plenty, actually. Extensive evidence shows that winning streaks don't last very long. Yes, Bill Miller of Legg Mason famously beat the S&P 500 index for fifteen years running, but his feat was only extraordinary because he was the only active manager ever to have done so. A typical outperformer will rise to the top for six months, a year—perhaps even two years. After that, the limelight shifts to a new star, and the old market favorite can't outpace the index anymore. But investors are reluctant to give up on a fund that has done well for them. They hang on until they are experiencing losses, and only then do they sell—while incurring fees and taxes—and go off in search of the next pair of hot hands. It's illogical, costly, and frustrating.

There is another issue with active investing that doesn't get discussed enough. Many managers play games with their portfolios and the benchmark against which they measure their performance. They'll pick a straw-man benchmark such as the S&P 500, then invest in volatile, riskier stocks that aren't even part of that index but that they figure will help them beat the benchmark. For example, sometimes a manager who really should measure himself against a US small-cap value index (such as the Russell 2000 value index) because he is investing in US small-cap value stocks will use the S&P 500 as his benchmark. Remember from chapter 3 that small company and value stocks have historically performed better than large-cap and growth stocks because they are riskier investments. So what the active manager is doing is taking on more risk by investing in small and value stocks but comparing himself to the S&P 500, which is not as risky—the straw-man problem. This straw-man problem is pervasive in the media where pundits will talk about it being a "stock picker's market" for a change. What they really should say is that value stocks and small company stocks are in favor now, taking the place of the US large company stocks that had been in favor in recent years. Sure, it's easier to "beat the market" when you take on more risk than the market you're trying to beat or when the asset class you invest in (e.g., small-cap value stocks) happens to be in favor now and the benchmark you are comparing yourself to is out of favor now.

In contrast to active management, indexing—a strategy that's also known as "passive" investing—is not only more likely to earn you a better return, it also simplifies your life to a remarkable degree. If you want to buy a stock, you can choose from among those issued by no fewer than 4,000 publicly traded companies—in the United States alone! And that figure has actually *declined* in recent years. Assembling a portfolio out of so many individual stocks could drive you crazy by forcing you to delve into the valuation of each one. Doing all that work is a waste of your precious time and money, which is why investing in index funds is my Third Fundamental. With a single decision, you can acquire exposure to a broad swathe of the market. Better still, you'll save a lot on fees and cut out various kinds of risk along the way. This is one of those rare occasions when being passive, and spending *less* time on your portfolio, will actually produce the best investment outcome for you. I love it when I can save both money and precious time!

It may seem counterintuitive that I'm suggesting you do less work rather than more, but the numbers tell the story. In early 2015 research firm DALBAR found that had investors just bought and held the stocks in the S&P 500 index (through an S&P 500 index fund), they would have fared better than they would have investing in actively managed mutual funds for all time periods studied—one year, three years, five years, a decade, two decades, and even three decades. Over the thirty-year period, investors would have earned an average annual return of 3.79 percent from investing in actively managed equity funds but 11.06 percent from investing in the S&P 500.[2]

You'd think that with such stark and consistent data, investors would have learned their lesson by now and stopped buying and selling actively managed funds instead of using index funds. But that would assume investors—who are human—behave rationally, and as the study of behavioral finance has shown us, they are nothing of the kind. One of the many ways we kid ourselves when it comes to managing money is by believing that, in spite of all the evidence to the contrary, we have some kind of spidey sense or superpower that will tell us how we can beat the odds and beat the market. Despite the fact that there has only ever been one person in the world with Bill Miller's stock-picking prowess—and that is Bill Miller himself—we believe we will somehow be the exception to the rule. Tragically for our self-delusions, academics who study winning streaks like Miller's suggest they have more to do with luck than anything else. One 2010 University of Chicago analysis found most managers don't possess the ability to generate enough profits even to cover their costs.[3] And Bill Gross, a noted bond money manager, commented during the twelfth year of Miller's winning streak, "Anyone can theoretically roll twelve sevens in a row." (Gross apparently didn't see the irony in his statement given that he himself was, and remains, an active investor and not an index manager.)

You don't have to look to the world of professional investors to find examples of this fallacy. Maggie, a woman I know, was caught up with a number of other investors in an actively managed fund that had a great track record for ten years. The fund looked wonderful based on that track record. But what neither Maggie nor most of her fellow investors realized at the time was that virtually all that wonderful performance came from a single stock, Qualcomm.

The manager had done a great job buying and selling Qualcomm at the right times—buying it low and selling it high to capture as many gains as possible. But as more time passed after he had sold the Qualcomm shares, the fund manager had to start reporting track records for periods that no longer included these gains. First the three-year performance didn't look so good, because it had been more than three years since the fund had benefited from that Qualcomm trade. Then the five-year performance didn't look so good, because it had now been five years since the trade. Then eventually it had been more than ten years and the fund's performance looked mediocre at best. The more years that went by without Qualcomm stock's blockbuster gains boosting the portfolio, the clearer it became that the manager really wasn't so brilliant after all. He'd benefited from one good stock pick, but was unable to repeat that success. As his

investors started to sell because of the deteriorating track record, the manager had to sell holdings. That, in turn, created
taxable events for investors in the fund. Gradually, many of the
investors ended up selling the fund, paying all the taxes, and
moving on to look for the next hot manager, again based on a
past track record that likely would not repeat itself.

This pattern is consistent over a wide range of funds. Every
study I've seen on the correlation between mutual funds that did
well in the past with mutual funds that do well in the future has
shown that there is no correlation you can count on. For example, one study showed that, "Out of the 687 funds that were in
the top quartile as of March 2012, only 3.78 percent managed to
stay there by the end of March 2014."[4] This is why every single
advertisement you'll see for a mutual fund carries some version
of the same disclaimer: "Past performance does not guarantee future results." Of course, this will usually be buried somewhere in
the fine print or spoken rapidly at the end of an audio ad, but it's
probably the most important honest information in the ad. No
manager in his right mind is going to confess that he has little
chance of outperforming an index fund, but now that you know
the truth, I hope you'll resist these marketing efforts in favor of
your own common sense: invest in index funds.

Indexing Is Catching On

Indexing may once have been known as Bogle's Folly, but in the
decades since it was introduced, it has won over fans in some
unlikely places. Peter Lynch, a legendary stock picker who for-
merly managed the Magellan Fund for Fidelity Investments—
one of the iconic actively managed funds—has remarked that in

spite of "all the time and effort that people devote to picking the next fund, the hot hand, the great manager," the results have, for the most part, produced "no advantage."

And if being able to purchase a portfolio that gives you exposure to a wide swathe of investments without having to worry about whether or not a manager is going to lose his or her touch next month isn't enough of an inducement, then consider the fees. Index funds are the cheapest products you can invest in, bar none, and (as I'll demonstrate when we get to the Fifth Fundamental) keeping fees low is one of the surest ways to protect your wealth. Index funds can keep their fees low because they are tracked to an existing index—meaning the person designing the fund doesn't have to research which stocks to include; she just uses the ones listed in that particular index. From there, constructing the fund itself is relatively simple. For instance, if we're looking at an S&P 500 fund, and if Apple's stock makes up 3.57 percent of the S&P 500, then the fund company will try to make sure its index fund's assets are invested so as to track Apple's performance with 3.57 percent of the portfolio. The fund company doesn't recruit high-priced research "talent" to try to second-guess the market and decide whether Apple's earnings will disappoint investors this quarter, triggering a sell-off in the stock. The money the company saves by not having to pay for these analysts is then passed on to investors in the form of lower fees. Where an active manager might charge 1 percent or more of your assets to manage your portfolio, Vanguard charges a mere five cents for every $100 you invest, or 0.05 percent.

When you consider all that you get for that miniscule fee, it's kind of miraculous. Whatever segment of the economy starts booming next, you'll be participating, but your returns won't ever be totally dependent on a single sector to the extent that it will wreak havoc on your portfolio.

For all the new supporters indexing has attracted over the last forty years, it still has its detractors. Many crafty opponents may have accepted (reluctantly) that indexing works in the US large company market (e.g., the S&P 500) because it's so large, actively traded, and efficient. They insist, though, that other markets are just, well, *different*. You'll hear them argue that shares of small companies have lighter trading volumes, and that makes indexing tougher. Or that it's still possible for stock pickers to make money overseas because foreign markets are less actively traded and thus less efficient, leaving more room for someone who does lots of research to profit from their own clever ideas. Active investing, proponents insist, is especially fruitful in emerging markets, which are so unpredictable that careful stock picking is the only way to prevent your portfolio of emerging market investments from blowing up in your face.

The problem with these seemingly perspicacious arguments is that, in fact, indexing trumps stock picking in all these markets. William Sharpe, a famous financial markets expert, explained why, noting that indexing's rewards don't have anything to do with how efficient a market is (in other words, how active the trading is, how many participants there are, and so on) but depend on the laws of mathematics, and specifically on the question of cost. According to Sharpe, "After costs, the average passive investor must outperform the average active investor."[5] In contrast, a manager who picks stocks starts out at an automatic disadvantage thanks to his high cost structure. These costs will likely be even higher for an international fund—because there's more expensive research involved, suggesting that, in fact, index funds are the better option. Sure, you might pay higher fees for an emerging markets index fund or a small-cap US equity index fund than you would for the ultra-cheap S&P 500 fund (0.08 percent to 0.75 percent, compared to 0.05 percent), but these are still a lot less pricey than their actively managed counterparts, which usually charge more than 0.50 percent, and many times more than 1 percent.

Only a small number of active managers are likely to beat the odds and beat the index. Indeed, the data (as seen in Figure 4.1) shows that during the five years that ended in December 2012, 76 percent of actively managed emerging markets funds failed to beat their index. A hefty 74 percent of international active funds flunked this test, as did 62 percent of global stock funds; and an astonishing 83 percent of small-cap and 90 percent of mid-cap US stock funds also fell short of the mark. Indexing won that round, hands down.

Index funds, in addition to being cheap and efficient, will also help you stick to your long-term asset-allocation plan when the market becomes stormy. The key is to identify index funds that will track those different asset classes of your predetermined asset-allocation plan. So if you have decided to invest 5 percent of your assets in US small-cap value stocks, do some research [Google is a great place to start—type the name of the category of fund you're looking for in the search box (e.g. "US small cap value index fund"), and see what comes up], and look for a fund that specializes in that asset class. Often, the name will give you a hint [for example, Vanguard Total Stock Mkt Idx (VTSMX) for the whole US stock market, Vanguard FTSE Developed Markets Index ETF (VEA) for Vanguard's developed international stock index fund, or Vanguard FTSE Emerging Markets Index ETF

Active Management Just Doesn't Work—Anywhere

Percentage of Active Public Equity Funds That Failed to Beat the Index
Five Years as of December 2012

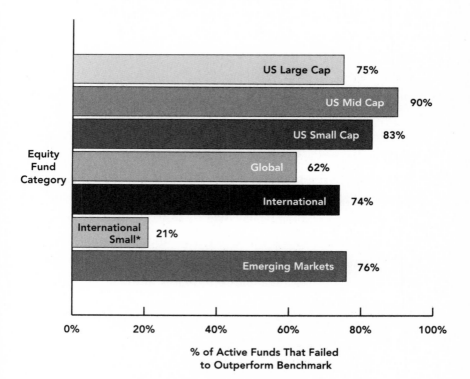

*The reason this is lower is due to the fact that these active managers actually had significant holdings in emerging market stocks, which is a different asset class, therefore being compared to the wrong benchmark!

Figure 4.1

(VWO) for Vanguard's emerging markets index fund]. If not, Google it and see whether it describes itself as an index fund. If it doesn't, toss it to one side. If it is an index fund, then look up more information online with Morningstar, the mutual fund research company. Pay particular attention to the Morningstar "style box" (also called style map)—a three-by-three box matrix that summarizes the qualities of every mutual fund the firm analyzes. It will tell you how Morningstar defines the fund—the top right corner is a large-cap growth fund, the bottom left corner is a small-cap value, and any funds that occupy the middle box are mid-cap blend funds.

When you're looking at the style box, pay attention to where the dot representing the fund in question lies. Is it right in the heart of the box for small-cap value, or in the top corner of the box, where it might be closer to a different category of fund? I also like to check Morningstar data to see what fees different index funds are charging. I make sure the fund I'm interested in has been around for years and that it is large enough (hundreds of millions and preferably billions of dollars in the fund) that I can trade its shares without any problems. Look at the top of the Morningstar Quote page (see next page) to find the size of the fund. Most of Vanguard's index funds (both mutual funds and ETFs) and Blackrock's iShares index ETFs meet my criteria.

Once you have found an index fund that looks as if it meets all your criteria, you can buy it using whatever portion of your portfolio you want in that asset class. Let the index take care of the rest.

Fees

Size of Fund

Style Box

Figure 4.2

Some More Guidance on
Choosing Index Funds

I've already given you some ideas about how to set about identifying the right funds for your needs with the help of Google and Morningstar. But choosing the right funds to suit your needs will depend on how much you have to invest to start. If you don't have a lot of money to spare and are just building your portfolio, look for broad index funds rather than trying to buy a lot of individual positions to match each of the asset classes in which you want to invest. For example, look for a fund that gives you exposure to the whole US stock market and to all international markets, or even to the global stock market. Then if you want to overweight certain asset classes (such as small-cap value stocks), you can buy an additional specialty fund to complement those broad, "master" index funds. As your portfolio grows, you can fine-tune your asset allocation by investing directly in each asset class in the percentage that you want (remember how detailed the examples of target allocations became at the end of the last chapter?).

Unfortunately, it may not always be plain sailing if you're trying to do this under the umbrella of a retirement plan administered by your company. Sadly, too many corporate retirement plans lack a wide range of options for index funds. Of course, almost everyone these days provides the plain vanilla S&P 500 fund, but if you're looking for an index fund to get exposure to US small company stocks or international stocks, you may come up empty. If this is the case, try urging your company to add a broader array of index funds to its list of offerings—e.g., Vanguard or Dimensional Fund Advisor (DFA) funds, both of which offer a variety of low-cost index funds. DFA funds are not available directly to retail investors (you have to go through an approved adviser or through your company), so having the option to buy them through your company would be a great benefit.

If instead of a company retirement account you've opened your own individual retirement account—for example, an IRA or Roth IRA—or if you're investing other assets outside a tax-sheltered retirement plan, you'll have more freedom to choose your own investments. So look for index funds for the asset classes you want to invest in.

Exchange-Traded Funds (ETFs)

For standard indices such as the S&P 500 or the Russell 2000 (which captures the performance of US small company stocks), there are comparable ETFs available. However, sometimes only a mutual fund will give you exposure to the particular market segment you are seeking. For instance, I like using the index funds offered by DFA when I'm making an allocation to small company stocks and value stocks for my clients, because DFA, in my view, does a better job of capturing exposure to very small companies and delving more deeply into value territory. That means that with those products I get more of what I'm looking for: small stock exposure with a value tilt.

If you have a choice, though, take the time to try to figure out which of these options will be the least expensive for you to buy and own. Google information on both the mutual fund and the ETF to find out what the internal ongoing management fees of each are. Also consider how much you'll have to pay in the form of trading fees or other costs to purchase either. It's free to buy some mutual funds and ETFs at certain discount brokerage firms, but in other instances, it will cost you more to buy mutual funds than it would to purchase ETFs, because ETFs trade like a stock and you can buy any number of shares for a flat rate of less than $10. (For example, as I write this, Fidelity's flat rate for a trade is only $4.95.)

If you are investing money in a taxable account rather than a retirement account, and if you have a choice between purchasing a mutual fund or an ETF that indexes the same part of the market, tax reasons usually favor buying the ETF. When you invest in a mutual fund, you are purchasing a pool of stocks alongside other investors, which can have some unfortunate tax consequences. If some of your fellow investors in that pool decide to sell, you will be "mutually" sharing the capital gains their decisions trigger that year, even if you don't sell your own shares in the mutual fund, which means you will have to pay taxes on your share of those gains when those other investors sell. In contrast, when you purchase an ETF, you buy your own basket of stocks and generally won't have to pay capital gains until you sell your own shares. Also, ETFs have a way to limit capital gains when they rebalance internally that doesn't apply to mutual funds, so ETFs are more tax-efficient than mutual funds for this reason as well. Owning ETFs is a tax win.

If you decide to purchase an index fund in the form of an ETF, and find yourself having to decide between various ETFs that track the same index, there is another cost to consider. Look at the spread, or the difference between what it costs to buy a share of the ETF and what it costs to sell the same share. The market maker, whose role is to facilitate market transactions, takes a small portion of the share price of both purchases and sales, creating a spread. If that spread is more than a penny or two, see if you can find an ETF with a narrower spread; that's a better product, because it offers you more liquidity. The more liquidity the better; you want that spread to be as tiny as possible, because that means the smallest amount possible of your money is going to traders in the form of a fee, and the largest amount possible is being invested. The liquidity of a fund usually is linked to its size (the amount of assets it is managing), and you can easily turn to Morningstar's website to find this (and a lot more) information.

Entertainment Accounts for Those Who Still Want to Pick Stocks

Embracing indexing doesn't mean you can't have some fun from time to time . . . if your version of fun involves picking stocks. I will occasionally encounter a client who gets an adrenaline rush from stock picking or is sort of addicted to watching CNBC and trying to figure out when to jump in and out of the market's turmoil. For people who like this kind of excitement, I'm a fan of what I call "entertainment accounts," if only as a relief valve for people who just can't let go of their passion for stock picking or market timing. Clients who have these accounts usually keep a fraction of their investments in them. Managing this money takes up a lot of their time, but it seems to satisfy their craving to see whether they can beat the market. It's actually a kind of therapy. I even have one of these accounts myself!

Ironically, though, the reason I advocate for entertainment accounts is because mine has taught me an important lesson:

despite my financial training, experience, and time I spend focused on the markets, I don't do any better managing money this way (and I usually do worse) than I do when I invest the lion's share of my portfolio in index funds and leave it alone. On the rare occasions that I do better than a portfolio of index funds, the returns haven't been worth the time or energy I've spent trying to generate them. So my entertainment account ultimately isn't very entertaining. And usually my clients with entertainment accounts eventually reach the same conclusion.

What About Concentrated Bets on Individual Stocks?

You may have heard of some people who got extremely rich by taking what are known as concentrated risks. This is what happened, for example, when individuals with the right connections (and a healthy appetite for risk) invested in Facebook when it was little more than a dorm-room start-up run by a nerdy Harvard student named Mark Zuckerberg. These early investors earned a far, far greater return on their investments than those who waited to buy stock until Facebook was a proven business with many millions of dollars of revenues and more than a billion users worldwide. Venture capitalists and other professional investors can make a fortune by concentrating their money in a handful of very risky bets like that. Of course, only a few start-ups go on to achieve the level of success Facebook has, and most end up failing within the first few years. So while the potential for reward is greater the bigger the more concentrated risk you take, so is the potential for it all to turn sour.

That kind of investing—swinging for the fences with highly concentrated risky investments—is strictly for those who are trying to make a fortune quickly and in a high-risk way. It should not be a part of your investment strategy if you are simply trying to generate the best return possible over the long term while also preserving your wealth. Investing the slow and steady way, by following the Five Fundamentals, means that while you won't become a millionaire overnight, you also won't end up distracted from what really matters in your day-to-day life—your family, your job, your pastimes—because you're worried about losing it all. You don't have to pay attention to every little success or misstep a particular company makes or constantly be on the hunt for new potential winners so you can get in on the ground floor. The strategy afforded by the Five Fundamentals allows you to make smaller bets on a large number of stocks through index funds.

So sure, you might want to own stakes in Amazon and Netflix because they are two of the hottest digital companies around, but you'll also want to invest in cable, telephone, and entertainment companies as the way we consume our video content continues to change. As that landscape shifts, which companies will be the big winners and which will fall behind? I don't want to predict; I do want to make sure my clients profit from the changes by owning the asset class through a broad variety of companies in index funds.

What About the Sentimental Value of Some Individual Stocks I Inherited?

I've noticed that some people who inherit stocks from a parent, grandparent, or other loved one want to hang on to the shares because they have some sentimental attachment—it's as if those stocks somehow embody their relative. For example, a friend of mine named Vicky inherited stock in an oil company from her grandfather. She knew nothing about the oil company but figured if her grandfather had chosen it, it must be worth keeping, and moreover, it reminded Vicky of him. Flash forward years later, and that oil company was in the news for not complying with regulations. The stock had never really done that well in the years since Vicky inherited it, but now it plummeted. My friend finally sold the stock, wishing she had not held on to it in the first place. So if you have sentimental attachment to your inherited stocks, take a photo of the statement, and then frame the photo if you wish, but then, after discussing the tax consequences of selling with your CPA or other tax adviser, come up with a plan to sell the stocks themselves and put the money to work according to the Five Fundamentals. Your relative would be proud of you for investing the money wisely for the long run!

After I make my case for index funds, investors often ask me: "What would happen if everyone started using index funds?" These people worry that if everyone starts using index funds no one will be making sure the markets are efficient by doing the research to price stocks correctly according to their real value. As the data I cited earlier shows, with only about 23 percent of US mutual fund money currently invested in index funds, we're so far away from that point that we needn't fret about it. (Some have even argued that having 80 percent of all the money in the market in index funds would be OK because we only need about 20 percent of the money in the market to be actively managed to keep the markets efficient.[6]) So rather than worry that too many investors are catching on to the benefits of indexing, be glad you are one of them and that others, who are paying a lot for active management, are keeping the markets efficient for you so you can use index funds.

Plus it's safe to say that actively managed funds will continue to be much more heavily marketed than index funds. Brokers and certain kinds of financial advisers make a lot of money peddling actively managed funds. The companies that offer these actively managed funds budget some of the higher fees they charge investors for marketing expenses. The marketing efforts also help fund companies get their actively managed products into company-sponsored 401(k) plans, which allows them to win even more investors that way. Index funds have to battle those headwinds, along with our own internal behavioral biases. We just don't want to believe we can't pick stocks.

Indexing may not be sexy or exciting. But you don't want a sexy and exciting investment portfolio, because they are fickle friends and can leave you heartbroken. You're much better off with a portfolio that is disciplined and rational. Indexing is a system you can understand on an intellectual level and one you can stick to without much effort. Think of your portfolio as you would a partner. It might be fun to have a hot, unpredictable fling, but if you're going to depend on someone over the long haul—for twenty, thirty, forty, or more years—you want someone stable, someone you can understand and trust, not someone you constantly have to worry about being erratic. So if you really love your money, put it in an index fund and kiss it good night.

5

THE FOURTH FUNDAMENTAL
Rebalance Regularly

Perhaps you've caught a glimpse somewhere—in a design magazine or in a display of folk art—of what are known as crazy quilts. These bed coverings are made of scraps of cloth of every kind, from brightly colored velvets to dingy sacking materials—whatever the women who made them had on hand. The result is a random mishmash of colors and shapes with no discernable pattern.

When anyone captures the performance of various asset classes, year after year, in some kind of image, the lack of rhyme and reason in the picture that emerges (as you can see in the chart in Figure 5.1 that follows) bears a resemblance to a crazy quilt. Except that while a quilter might find joy and creativity in this kind of randomness, investors are likely to respond to this bewildering unpredictability with frustration or even denial.

Investment Returns Are Random: Diversification and Rebalancing Are Keys to Success

Annual returns (%): 2001–2015

You never know which markets will outperform from year to year.

By holding a globally diversified portfolio, investors are positioned to capture returns wherever they occur.

	2001	2002	2003	2004	2005	2006	2007	2008	2009	2010	2011	2012	2013	2014	2015
Higher Return	12.3	7.6	62.6	33.2	34.5	36.0	39.8	8.8	79.0	28.1	9.4	18.6	38.8	32.0	5.8
	8.4	5.1	56.3	29.9	25.5	32.6	8.2	6.6	51.4	26.9	3.4	17.9	32.4	13.7	4.5
	7.3	3.6	47.3	26.0	13.8	19.8	6.3	4.7	28.5	24.9	2.3	17.1	26.0	4.9	1.4
	6.4	3.4	36.2	18.3	4.9	18.4	5.9	-33.8	27.2	19.2	2.1	16.3	1.2	1.9	1.0
	2.5	-6.0	28.7	10.9	4.6	15.8	5.5	-37.0	26.5	15.1	0.6	16.0	0.6	1.2	0.9
	-2.4	-7.1	2.0	2.7	3.1	4.3	3.6	-39.2	2.3	3.7	-4.2	2.1	0.3	0.2	0.2
	-10.2	-20.5	1.9	1.3	2.4	4.1	-1.6	-47.8	0.8	2.0	-15.5	0.9	-0.1	-1.8	-4.4
Lower Return	-11.9	-22.1	1.5	0.8	1.3	3.8	-17.6	-53.2	0.2	0.8	-18.2	0.2	-2.3	-5.0	-14.6

Figure 5.1

- ■ S&P 500 Index
- ■ Russell 2000 © Index
- ■ Dow Jones US Select REIT Index
- ☐ Dimensional International Small Cap Index
- ▨ MSCI Emerging Markets Index (gross div.)
- ▨ BofA Merrill Lynch One-Year US Treasury Notes Index
- ▨ Bloomberg Barclays US Treasury 1–5 Yr. Total Return Index
- ▨ Citi World Government Bond 1–5 Years Index (currency-hedged in USD terms)

Go on, take a look at the chart carefully. Every shade represents a different asset class, and each column represents a different year. The top row indicates the best-performing asset class for that particular year, while the bottom represents the worst. For example, in 2001 the best-performing asset class was real estate (the Dow Jones REIT index), which gained 12.3 percent. The worst was the S&P 500, which lost 11.9 percent. But overall in the fifteen columns, representing fifteen years' worth of data, can you find any kind of pattern?

I suspect you can't. I certainly can't, because there really isn't one: it's just as the shades suggest, a crazy quilt, with a random distribution of returns. Yes, each shade is represented once in each column, but that's the only pattern—and that's only because each asset class continues to exist from one year to the next. Beyond that? There's no relationship between what did well one year and what outperformed the following year.

That is because financial markets, like life itself, are subject to random forces. You can try to impose order on them by guessing what will do well next year or the year after that, but you'll fail, and in the process, you'll compromise your attempts to improve your finances. That's why being disciplined and sticking to your original asset allocation is the best plan.

That's why the Fourth Fundamental involves rebalancing your portfolio at least once a year, selling a portion of each of your relative winners and buying more of those asset classes that have not done as well, so that you maintain that all-important asset allocation we discussed in chapter 3.

I'll get around to the mechanics of how to accomplish this later on in the chapter, but first let's review some of the reasons rebalancing is so essential, and why failing to rebalance can leave you with a problematic portfolio. The actual process of re-balancing may take you only a few hours once a year if you do it yourself (and no time at all if you are paying a financial adviser to oversee your portfolio), and while it may seem daunting at first, the fact that you already have a target asset-allocation plan will help you see exactly what you need to do. So when you're inevitably tempted to stray—to hold on to an asset class that has been outperforming or to sell off an asset class that hasn't done as well as the rest—just remember that, as the preceding chart shows, the only pattern that exists in the market is the fact that there is no pattern.

Pundits, of course, will try to convince you otherwise. Many members of this group have a lot to gain—in prestige or financially—from persuading you that they have some special insight, that they can decipher some hidden code in the crazy quilt. But as I've shown you time and again throughout this book, the market inevitably gets the last laugh.

The plain truth is that markets are unpredictable, and sooner or later that unpredictability will catch up with those investors who think they can outwit market forces. Those who were around back in the mid to late 1990s may remember the era that one Goldman Sachs strategist referred to as "the Goldi-locks economy"—not too hot or too cold, but just right—and the bull market in technology stocks spawned by the Internet rev-olution. Everything was going great—until it wasn't, and most prognosticators did not anticipate the sell-off that followed.

Or consider what the preceding chart tells us about real estate. If you had invested in real estate investment trusts, also known as REITs, an investment product tied to property that generates income and is generally seen as a window into the health of the real estate market as a whole, you would have earned 36 percent in 2006. In fact, you probably would have been breaking out the champagne, because that would have been the third time in four consecutive years that this asset class had generated returns of more than 30 percent. By that point, investors like you might have drawn one of two conclusions: 1) "Hmm, clearly momentum favors this group so I should get in on the action and add to my holdings!" or 2) "Gulp! A lot of money has been made here in a relatively short amount of time. I've made a lot of money already, so perhaps it's time to take some of my chips off the table." Regardless of which category you fell into, you probably wouldn't have predicted that real estate was heading for an unprecedented, apocalyptic sell-off. The real estate asset class plunged 17.6 percent in 2007, making it the worst-performing category, and it nosedived 39.2 percent in 2008, when it had plenty of competition for the title of worst performer in that year of the financial crisis.

So without looking at the chart, consider how you may have felt about investing in real estate in 2009. Might you have been optimistic, thinking the real estate market had probably bottomed out and was now ready for a rally? Or would you have written it off as a toxic asset class and opted to invest your money elsewhere?

If you had assumed the latter, you would have been kicking yourself the following year. In 2009 real estate returned 28.5 percent, and by 2010 it was once again the top-performing asset class, with a 28.1 percent return. What a roller-coaster ride! Had you jumped off midway through—had you decided not to maintain your allocation to real estate at its target level, say— you would have missed all that upside.

If investors know something about a stock or a bond or other market security, its price reflects that piece of information. Are people afraid that a pharmaceutical company's research and development pipeline is running dry? If that's the case, its stock will have already begun to slide in response to that anxiety. So when markets move sharply and asset classes start delivering different returns relative to each other (when one of those boxes slides higher or lower in its column on the crazy quilt), it's because something has happened suddenly that has surprised everyone in the market. China announces unexpectedly bad economic data—and the ripple effects send emerging markets sharply lower. Apple or another big company announces poor sales or low profits and ignites a wave of selling in its shares. Perhaps investors start to assume this company's disappointing results send a broader signal about the overall economy, and the sell-off spreads to all US large-cap stocks. The Federal Reserve is expected to raise interest rates but doesn't, sending bond investors into a tizzy.

It should go without saying that no one can predict surprises. And in order to design next year's column in the crazy quilt correctly, you would have to predict not just one surprise event but *all* of them. On top of that, you'd have to be able to gauge how the market will respond to each of these events. Anyone can see that's an impossible task, but somehow that doesn't stop people from trying. Remember, I'm here to help you build your savings over the long run, and to transform it into wealth: wealth that will enable you to fulfill your dreams for yourself and those you love, and ensure you are financially secure. That's not a goal that can be accomplished through gambling. (In fact, investing is much better than gambling because the odds are with you when you invest in the stock markets for the long run, but they are against you in casinos, where the odds favor the house.)

Rebalancing your portfolio to maintain your target asset allocation is the best possible way to ensure that you never end up betting too much on any single one of those asset classes in the crazy quilt chart—that you don't end up overinvesting in something that is about to go bust or underinvesting in something that is about to start outperforming. Your asset allocation may be the most critical decision you make, but it won't work as it's designed to if you don't check it and correct it as needed. Imagine, for a moment, that you had a 10 percent stake in real estate in 2000 that you had allowed to remain unadjusted between then and 2007. Several years of gains of 30 percent or more would have meant that by the time the market tanked in 2007 you would have had significantly more than 10 percent of your assets in this one class—and would therefore have been much more exposed to the bloodshed that followed than you would have been had you stuck with your original 10 percent. This, of course, would have significantly damaged your portfolio. The same applies to US large-cap stocks in the years leading up to the dot-com bubble. Indeed, for pretty much every asset class, I can point to a period of prolonged outperformance that has ended in a sudden slump. Anyone leaving their asset allocation as the markets moved it, letting one asset class balloon when it was in favor without rebalancing it, would have suffered disproportionately when the slump came. And of course, if you did this with one asset class, the odds probably are that you allowed it to happen with others—being underexposed to an asset class that is about to have great performance, for instance.

You need to have the discipline to hit the reset button every so often and evaluate how you are actually invested, because over time a series of these relative movements can end up significantly distorting your portfolio, to the point that it bears little resemblance to the ideal asset allocation you drew up so carefully when you designed your investment program. When you did so, as we discussed in chapter 3, you paid careful attention to factors such as your investment objectives, the benefits of diversification, and your risk tolerance. You don't want to suddenly wake up one morning to discover your sliver of exposure to emerging markets has become gargantuan, or that your bond exposure has dwindled to nearly nothing and you've lost your safe haven against the volatility from the emerging markets.

That's why rebalancing is crucial. It's also a very straightforward process that should only take up a few hours of your time once a year. And all you have to do is redistribute your money from those segments of your portfolio that have outperformed to those that have been laggards in order to ensure that you retain the original exposure you wanted.

This may sound like a more daunting process than it actually is. Let's say your target allocation was 60 percent stocks and 40 percent bonds, but that over the course of the year the stock market has gone up more than bonds have, thus shifting your weightings of each class. As a result, you now have 63 percent stocks and 37 percent bonds. To get this back to your target 60/40 split, simply sell some of the stock index funds in your portfolio, and use the proceeds to add to your holdings of bonds or bond index funds. Because, for all the reasons we discussed in the last chapter, you're investing in index funds, you simply sell some of one index fund in one asset class and

You know it's time to rebalance when:

- You have 10 percent more (or less) in stocks than your target allocation suggests you should. For instance, if your goal is to have 60 percent in stocks and 40 percent in bonds, and your current breakdown is 66 percent in stocks and 34 percent in bonds, it's time to reallocate, selling stocks and buying bonds.

- You have 25 percent more (or less) in any individual asset class than your target allocation. Let's say you want to have 10 percent in US small company stocks but your allocation has fallen to 7.25 percent. It's time to buy more to bring the total back up to 10 percent; to finance that, sell whatever is now overweight in your target allocation, or has gone up, relative to small stocks.

- You haven't rebalanced in the last twelve months.

use the proceeds to buy more of the funds you already have in the asset class that is currently underweight. I've given you an example involving only two asset classes, but the principle holds true across as many as you have in your portfolio.

Because all movements in your portfolio must be relative, it's pretty easy to accomplish this. If you have two asset classes in your portfolio, and asset class A goes up as a percentage of your portfolio, then mathematically asset class B *must* decline in size. So if there are five asset classes, if three go up in percentage terms, the other two, by definition, must have declined in percentage terms. And to rebalance, you'll be selling some of the holdings in those three winners to add to the positions in the two relative losers.

When I rebalance my clients' portfolios, I typically choose to do so in November, unless the market has been very volatile and given me specific reasons to want to rebalance earlier. That gives me a specific time of year that is "rebalancing season"—and I like that discipline of having one specific period that I set aside to do this.

Rebalancing and Taxes

Another reason I like to rebalance in November is it helps me prepare myself and my clients for tax season. By November I'm already thinking about ways to minimize my clients' tax payments for the year, and rebalancing can play an important role in that process.

While you should discuss your own tax strategies with your adviser, when I review my clients' portfolios, especially later in the year, I want to find ways for them to generate losses. This may sound crazy at first. Why would anyone deliberately sell something to lose money? However, it's actually an established strategy known as tax-loss harvesting. When I sell securities in my clients' portfolios that generate a tax loss, that action reduces their net taxable gains for the year and therefore can lower the amount of taxes they have to pay. Because losses are only generated when you sell a position, I'll then use the proceeds from the sale to purchase, immediately, another very similar product so that my client remains invested. For instance, if my client owns the S&P 500 index, and the position has some losses when I go to rebalance, I might sell part or all of that position and buy a Russell 1000 Index fund to replace it, because the Russell 1000, like the S&P 500, invests in stocks of large US companies. (Securities laws bar me from selling something and buying the same thing again within a short period of time just to generate a tax loss—that's an abuse of the system.) My client then benefits on two fronts: she has captured a tax benefit and is still positioned to participate when the market eventually revives. If you don't have enough taxable gains and/or some income to match against all your losses in one year, the unused tax losses can be rolled over into future tax years.

This is a different kind of rebalancing, because it's to generate a tax advantage rather than to maintain an asset allocation, but it's worth watching out for and taking advantage of if you can. Finding losses gets harder with time, if you're not constantly investing new money, because most investments increase in value: the losses simply aren't there to harvest! But as long as you continue to put new savings into the market in taxable accounts, there will be short periods of time when the market dips that offer the opportunity to harvest a tax loss. I'd recommend you seek these out and try to keep your tax burden as low as possible. In addition to saving some money up front, you can also invest savings into the market, helping you reach your financial goals that much more rapidly.

I also prefer to rebalance portfolios around November because the period between May and November historically has been weaker for the stock market. This strategy allows you to take advantage of seasonal upturns that history has shown frequently occur in December and the beginning of the new year.

I know I can't time the markets, but that's not my goal. My objective is to rebalance, and because I'm doing that in November for tax purposes anyway, the fact that there's a seasonal trading pattern that may also benefit my clients is an added bonus.

When the market is extremely volatile, I don't confine myself to rebalancing once a year. I never want my clients' allocations to get too far out of whack. If the stock market has a bad year and sells off, that means that suddenly my clients aren't just going to be underweight in stocks, but will also likely have a big overweight position in fixed income. I want to bring both asset classes back into line with the asset-allocation model we have carefully designed. Frankly, if you want to rebalance every quarter, go for it. It can't hurt to make sure your portfolio matches your target allocation, but as long as you do it once a year, you will be far ahead of those who let the market determine how their portfolios look.

So if rebalancing can help keep you on track, why don't all investors do it regularly? I suspect it's like eating a balanced diet, getting physicals, visiting the dentist for cleanings, or exercising regularly: we all acknowledge it's important, even vital, but it feels like a chore. And yet, compared to going to the dentist or exercising, rebalancing is actually painless, can be relatively inexpensive (or even save you money on taxes if you are tax-loss harvesting, as described previously), and takes remarkably little time. And yet we seem to forget about it or don't make time to do it, procrastinating when we remember.

Then, of course, there's the psychological component that can often make rebalancing more difficult than it needs to be. Rebalancing requires us to fight our instincts, to refuse to succumb to the false conviction that our favored asset class—the one that has done so well in the last few years—is about to re-peat its performance. Don't fall into this group, please. Remem-ber, this book is about being a smart investor, and being smart requires discipline.

For a lesson in what can happen if you don't rebalance, let's consider a hypothetical investor named Mary. Mary started out with a portfolio of $100,000 and decided to allocate 60 percent of her assets to US large-cap stocks and 40 percent to US bonds. At the end of 2003, a year in which stocks did well, Mary saw that her investment in US large companies gave her a return of 28.7 percent. Mary was happy with this return and decided there was no reason to dump any of her equity holdings just so she could bolster her bond positions, which had generated less than a tenth of the returns that stocks did. So she let the position ride. And did so again in 2004, 2005, and 2006.

Failing to rebalance for the next four years left Mary with 70 percent of her portfolio in stocks by the end of 2007, and only 30 percent in US bonds, and a portfolio value of $156,770. That seems pretty good. But then along came the financial crisis of 2008, and with it a dramatic stock market sell-off that wiped out 37 percent of the value of the stock portion of her portfolio. So by the end of 2008, her portfolio was worth only $120,301.

What would have happened to Mary had she rebalanced in a disciplined fashion once a year? She would have main-tained her target exposure to stocks at 60 percent throughout, and by the end of 2008 she would have had a portfolio worth $125,763. Best of all, when she rebalanced again at the end of 2008—selling the bonds that had rallied, in favor of stocks that had slumped—very close to the point at which the stock market eventually would touch bottom the following March, she would have achieved the feat that almost no one accomplished: that of buying back into stocks when they were at their very cheapest. By the end of 2009, her portfolio would have been worth $145,859. In contrast, had she *not* rebalanced, but just let things ride, she still would have profited from that rebound—but would have finished 2009 with only $138,727 in her portfolio. Throughout the whole period, Mary also would have had a less volatile portfolio and the peace of mind that goes with knowing she never had much more than 60 percent of her portfolio exposed to the stock market, just as she had intended.

Stock pickers will brag about all the "smart" investments they've made over the years, but you'll be smarter just to stick with your asset allocation and rebalance regularly. And if you want to brag about it to all your friends, go ahead! You'll be doing them a favor, because you'll be showing them how pursuing a disciplined, commonsense strategy will enable them not only to resist market panics but also to capture tremendous market opportunities, buying in at the lowest levels in a decade. That's far more worthy of boasting about than whether or not you got shares of a hot new public offering, because it shows that you're smart in a repeatable, long-term way and not just benefiting from blind luck. That's worth sharing.

It's emotionally difficult to give up on your winners—ask any gambler. That's why it's easier if you make it part of an annual routine, so you know that once a year, at least, you'll simply be tweaking your portfolio until it's back to the asset allocation you decided upon when you were thinking calmly about what your long-term investment objectives are, and not in the heat of the moment when you are excited by the fact that your favorite asset class has done so well for you this year. I'm not suggesting that it's easy to resist the human instinct to buy what is already doing well in the market and avoid what is lagging, because it isn't. But you need to try, because the returns you're celebrating today could just as easily become the large losses you're lamenting tomorrow.

And if you don't believe me, go back and take another glance at that crazy quilt. How many casino chips would you care to bet that you know which colors will emerge on top for the coming calendar year? And are you willing to stake your own financial well-being on that bet? Right, I thought not. So fall in love with rebalancing, and not your latest winning asset class.

6

THE FIFTH FUNDAMENTAL
Keep Fees Low

If I stopped a random woman on the street and asked her what she thought the biggest controllable risk to her long-term portfolio potential was, I can almost guarantee she wouldn't guess the right answer. She might say it was the risk of being invested during a big market downturn, like the bursting of the dot-com bubble or the great recession of 2008. She might mention the possibility of being taken for a ride by a Ponzi schemer like Bernie Madoff, or investing in a fraudulent company or one that goes bankrupt. Perhaps she'd mention the risk of not investing at all—sitting on the sidelines and watching as the market goes up without her taking advantage and growing her assets.

If you have read the preceding chapters and implemented all the advice they contain, you are already addressing all those risks to the greatest extent possible. Yes, market declines come and go, but if you remain invested in a diversified portfolio of low-cost index funds and regularly rebalance, you ensure you'll always be in a position to profit from the upturns when they come. If you're following the Third Fundamental and sticking to index funds, there is no risk you'll end up in the clutches of a Bernie Madoff and his "proprietary" (in this case, downright illegal) investment strategies and products, because you'll be buying plain vanilla funds that trade in the public markets. And of course, you'll be staying invested at all times, because as I have stated throughout this book, that's the key to making money at all. As long as you invest, and stay invested, your returns keep compounding. The more time you have, the more you can reinvest those earnings and leverage the potential of your original assets.

But there is another risk, and it's one that almost no one ever seems to consider. The one most of us forget about until it's too late. It doesn't grab headlines in the same way a market crash or a renegade money manager might. But it can wreak havoc on how much money you end up with when you have to look at how your nest egg will provide for you and your family.

Fees. Even if you follow the other four fundamentals exactly as I advise, if you fail to follow the Fifth Fundamental—keep fees low—you risk forfeiting a significant portion of the wealth you will have accumulated over time. You will have to pay some fees—that's just the cost of doing business—but unlike in other industries, you don't necessarily get more for your money if you pay high fees to invest. And in most cases, you actually end up with less. As I discussed in chapter 4, actively managed funds often charge higher fees than index funds because the costs associated with managing them are so high. But these funds, over the long run, don't end up doing as well as the market, so you end up giving up more money than you would have had you stuck to the cheaper, more straightforward option. But fees can hide in all sorts of places, so it's important to be aware of them and to make sure you're not paying more than you need to be. That's why keeping fees low is the fifth, and final, fundamental.

There's a famous story about a visitor who made his way to New York more than a century ago. The visitor admired all the yachts moored in New York's harbor bought by the city's top brokers, paid for by the giant fees they earned giving advice to their clients. He turned to his guide and asked, "Where are the customers' yachts?" The joke, of course, is that the customers couldn't afford to buy any yachts after paying those fees and following the brokers' advice. (This story is what inspired former professional trader Fred Schwed to write his classic book about the investment industry, *Where Are the Customers' Yachts?: or A Good Hard Look at Wall Street.*)

In an effort to illustrate just how much fees can eat into your earnings, let's imagine a thirty-five-year-old woman with about $100,000 in assets. Using history as a guideline, it's fair to say this woman could expect to earn an average of 6.5 percent a year in her investment portfolio. If she pays 1 percent a year in fees, she will end up earning 5.5 percent a year instead of 6.5 percent, and within thirty years, her $100,000 will be worth almost $500,000—not too shabby. But if she ends up paying 2 percent a year in fees and therefore earns only 4.5 percent a year in returns, she will end up with only $375,000, paying more than 30 percent ($125,000) of the $400,000 profit she could have earned to fees. Take those fees up one more notch to 3 percent, and her $100,000 will grow to a mere $280,000 over the next thirty years. In other words, this woman will have forfeited *more than half her potential investment gains and almost half her ultimate potential wealth* by paying those extra two percentage points in fees! This is the downside of compounding.

The more money you have, the greater the potential wealth you will forfeit if you pay too much in fees. Take a look at the chart in Figure 6.1. If you have $1 million dollars and pay 3 percent in fees over thirty years, you will end up with roughly $2.8 million at the end of the day. If you only pay 1 percent, however, you'll end up with nearly $5 million. Maybe you're thinking, *I don't need $5 million to retire; $2.8 million would be more than fine with me!* That may be true, but think of all that you could do with that extra money! You could pay for education expenses for your family or provide for them in other ways in the future, even long after you're gone, start a foundation that supports a cause important to you, or invest in your best friend's brilliant business idea so she can get it off the ground. The point is: why forfeit money when you don't have to?

How to Determine Your Fees

There are many different kinds of fees you will pay while investing your money, including brokerage fees, product-management fees, and, if you work with an adviser, financial adviser fees.

Because there are so many kinds of fees, and they can come in layers, levied by different providers and charged in different ways, the best thing you can do is talk to your broker, adviser, 401(k) provider, or any other financial professional involved with helping you set up your portfolio, and ask them one simple question: "Can you please tell me all the fees I am paying to you and everyone else for investing my money?"

Fees Matter

Assumed 6.5% Annualized Return Over 30 Years

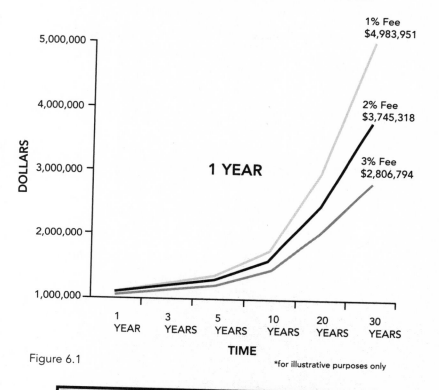

Figure 6.1

*for illustrative purposes only

- Over long time periods, high management fees and expenses can be a significant drag on wealth creation.

- Passive index investments generally maintain lower fees than the average actively-managed investment by minimizing trading costs and eliminating the costs of researching stocks.

- Fee-only advisers must act in your best interest (versus brokers).

If you ask your broker how much you're paying to invest in a particular mutual fund, and he tells you the management fees are 0.6 percent, ask him whether you also have to pay a load fee. This is a sales charge that can be applied when you either buy (a front-end load) or sell (a back-end load) the fund or have to pay every year for as long as you own the fund (a level

There are a host of different fees and other costs you can incur when investing. Some examples include the following:

Management Fee: Charged by a financial adviser, usually a percentage of assets. A management fee of more than 1 percent is too high, and as the assets in your portfolio grow, this fee should come down.

Underlying Fund Fees: The fund-management fees embedded in mutual funds or exchange-traded funds (ETFs). For index funds these should be less than 1 percent and usually fall between 0.05 percent and 0.5 percent. For actively managed funds, the fees are usually much higher.

Trading Costs: The cost of purchasing or selling ETFs and/or mutual funds on a brokerage platform. It can cost $10 or even less (Fidelity currently charges only load). The mutual fund world is so awash in excellent no-load funds that there's simply no point in buying funds that require investors to pay these load fees. So if you find out there is one on a fund you're investigating, say adios and find something else. You should also ask about any transaction fees, and how you will be paying your adviser. Make it *crystal* clear that you want

$4.95 per transaction, regardless of the number of shares being traded) to buy or sell an ETF position, because these trade like stocks, on exchanges. The fees for mutual fund transactions are usually higher (though some brokerage platforms offer no-cost-transaction mutual funds). Some fees may be $20 per trade; others may be double that.

Bid/Ask Spread: This is the difference between what you pay to buy a share of stock (such as an ETF position) and the price you would receive if you sold the same position. The more active the trading is in the particular ETF (or stock), the smaller the difference (or the narrower the spread). That's why it's usually a good idea to buy the most "liquid" (i.e., the most actively traded) ETFs, because the bid/ask spread will be as small as possible and you will lose as little as possible when buying or selling the position.

them to disclose every single kind of fee you will end up paying, regardless of who you are paying it to and what it's being paid for. Then add up these numbers and consider the results.

Some mutual fund companies can charge customers for expenses brokers incur in marketing their products, including some index funds. (These are known as 12b-1 fees.) Indeed, while Vanguard and most other index fund managers offer extremely low-fee funds—as should be the case for this type of product—other investment companies have, at times, charged as much as ten times what Vanguard has for nearly identical products. You can't afford simply to assume that a fund's fees must be low simply because it describes itself as an index fund.

You can't ignore the impact of smaller fees, either. Financial institutions might charge you an annual fee to serve as the custodian of your financial assets. There are wire transfer fees you can incur if you want to move money from one account to another. And your broker or banker might fail to pay you something that could benefit you, such as interest on any cash balances. If you buy a bond, rather than a bond mutual fund, you'll want to know how the dealer is marking up the bond price—but you may never be able to find out the exact fee, because that information is embedded in the bid/ask spread for the bond. If you think you're safe from fees because you're investing in a 401(k) plan, think again. You may be paying a share of the expenses for operating and administering the plan.

In addition to brokerage fees, you will pay fees to any adviser you hire to help you set up and manage your portfolio. A few different types of financial advisers exist, and they are usually described based on who pays for their services: you, or the companies whose financial products the adviser is paid for

Check Out the Fees Before You Decide Which Index Fund to Buy

Even Index Funds For the Same Index Can Have Different Fees

S&P 500 Index Fund Name	Symbol	Fee
iShares Core S&P 500	IVV	0.04%
Vanguard S&P 500 ETF	VOO	0.05%
Schwab® S&P 500 Index	SWPPX	0.09%
SPDR S&P® 500 ETF	SPY	0.10%
Shelton S&P 500 Index Direct	SPFIX	0.36%

selling. The best kind of advisers are "fee-only" advisers because the only fee they receive is a fully disclosed fee that you pay directly to them, usually a percentage of the assets you are investing. In other words, you, the investor, are the only one paying them, so the adviser has no incentive to offer you products from a third party that make him more money, but might not be best for your long-term wealth.

There are also "fee-based" advisers who, while collecting some or much of their income from fees directly from their clients, also receive commissions from insurance or investment firms when selling you products from these firms. That's a conflict of interest the adviser should disclose, though many do not.

The final type of adviser is commission-based. Traditionally known as brokers, these advisers earn all their income by selling you investment products and then receiving a commission from the companies that own these products. This may seem like a good deal because you're not paying much (if anything) up front for their services. But because they're getting paid commission, they have an incentive to sell you these products—even if they might not be the best for your needs. Essentially, they may seem like they are working for you, but they earn their living by doing what's best for the firms whose products they sell. That doesn't mean that there are not reputable commission-based brokers who want to do the best for their clients. It just means that you should be wary of the conflicts of interest with this business model and keep those conflicts in mind when deciding whether to invest in products with high fees recommended by advisers who are not fee-only.

The news these days might also give you reason to wonder about whether you are getting your money's worth from some of those product fees. In December 2015 JPMorgan Chase forked over $307 million to settle allegations that it improperly steered clients to some of its own products that carried higher fees and earned the bank more money than comparable rival products available for lower fees—even when those cheaper funds also had a better track record. Doing this allowed the bank to earn two sets of fees: an advisory fee for managing the clients' money and a management fee because they sold their clients the bank's own mutual fund. Regulators calculated that the deception—revealed by whistleblowers—cost the bank's clients about $127 million in excess fees. Banks can generally get away with this kind of behavior as long as they disclose that they have a conflict of interest, but regulators concluded that, in this case, JPMorgan Chase's disclosure wasn't adequate.

In spite of being called to task for this mishandling of client money, it is still perfectly legal for JPMorgan Chase and other banks to recommend their own products over others, even if those others have lower fees and better performance, as long as they clearly spell out any conflicts of interest. If this fact surprises or irks you, well, you're not alone. For nearly two decades, regulators have been trying to ensure everyone who provides Americans with financial advice is held to what is known as the fiduciary standard. Traditionally, only fee-only advisers (like myself) have been held to this standard, which requires them to put their clients' interests before absolutely anything else, including their own financial well-being. When I think of what it means to be a fiduciary, I try to imagine myself literally standing in my clients' shoes; then I decide what to do while viewing the situation from that perspective.

If you are working with a financial adviser and paying her a fee—however much it is—you want her to give you objective advice. To accomplish that, she should have an "open architecture" approach to business, meaning she can recommend any kind of investment product, from any provider—Vanguard, BlackRock's iShares, Dimensional Fund Advisors—for your portfolio, and select the product from the tool box that best meets your needs. Whenever a new client comes to me with a portfolio loaded, chock-a-block, with brand-name funds belonging to the brokerage firm of which they have been a client, I immediately become suspicious. It just doesn't seem likely that, out of all the thousands of possible choices in the asset classes in which my new client was investing, these proprietary funds were *really* the best possible options each and every time.

In April 2016 the Department of Labor, at the behest of President Obama, announced new rules that would govern how advisers have to treat a client's retirement funds. The rules, collectively known as the "Fiduciary Rule," would require anyone who manages retirement accounts to act as a fiduciary when managing these investments. This means they would have to avoid making misleading statements about the investments they recommend for a retirement savings account, ensure their fees are reasonable, and disclose basic information about any potential conflict of interest. Originally set to take effect in April 2017, at the time of this writing, the Trump Administration postponed their implementation, and it remains to be seen whether they will be implemented at all.

Of course, because these new rules would only apply to retirement accounts, we still have a long way to go before advocates of a new fiduciary standard are satisfied. In fact, the original retirement rule was meant to be more stringent but, thanks to Wall Street pushback, the Department of Labor eased some of the terms. For instance, while your adviser would have to act as a fiduciary and put your needs above all else when making specific recommendations about what to do with your IRA account, he could still talk to you about retirement planning in general without applying that standard. He could also continue to recommend house-brand mutual funds and annuities for your non-retirement accounts and continue collecting commissions on these products and simply sign a contract promising to act in your interests. There's a lot at stake, and even if the new, finicky rules are implemented, it's still going to be tough for a client to ensure she is being advised in the best possible manner. So the best thing you can do is to get educated in order to protect yourself.

The Role of a Fiduciary

Arguments over just who is a fiduciary and just what the term means have been going on for years. This used to be a straight-forward distinction because advisers and brokers were considered two different things and were therefore paid differently. Advisers did just what their moniker suggested and provided guidance, acting in the best interests of their clients, while brokers executed trades and solicited new accounts with the goal of boosting commission revenue for their own accounts and firms. These days, however, because anyone can call themselves an "adviser," and brokers and advisers generally boast similar credentials, ordinary investors may find it a lot harder to understand just where someone falls on this continuum. This is especially true because so many "advisers" have a penchant for weasel words and say things such as, "I act like a fiduciary." This is like saying, "I act like a doctor." You either are or you aren't. You can't be a fiduciary part of the time and not hold yourself to that standard the rest of the time. Being a fiduciary is a full-time gig. It has implications for the way you design your business, the kind of activities you will and will not undertake as a financial adviser, and the way you think about your clients.

You might imagine that with literally trillions of dollars in retirement savings at stake, even if advisers only capture a small fraction of the market, they'd earn enough to be happy without taking advantage of their clients and risking disciplinary hearings and fines by selling or marketing overpriced or underperforming funds. History shows that, too often, you'd be wrong.

So ask. Ask the adviser you are thinking of hiring to help you manage your investment portfolio whether she is a fiduciary. If she responds with weasel words, you need to dig deeper. Ask her which products her firm sells (if any), or if she earns a commission for selling you or her other clients any kinds of products (such as an insurance policy or an annuity). The first time she mentions that she or her colleagues sell anything, or that their firm is a "fee-based" advisory firm (as opposed to a "fee-only" business), it's time to flee. You may think selling insurance products—hey, they aren't really investments, are they?—isn't anything you need to worry about. But that's a sign that her firm has incentives to market high-cost products that will generate significant fees or commissions for the adviser, who in that case really is nothing more than a sophisticated broker or salesperson.

A fee-only adviser should be precisely that: someone who collects a single fee from a single source—her clients. There should be no confusion over where her loyalties lie. As a fiduciary, she should be able and willing to clarify just how she earns her compensation, and reassure you that none of it comes from product providers.

As the scrutiny over the link between fees and performance has mounted, Charles Schwab and TD Ameritrade have taken note. Starting in early 2016, both began offering to refund management fees to unhappy clients who had lost money in their managed accounts for two consecutive quarters. Schwab went further still with its "accountability guarantee," offering to re-fund a quarter's worth of fees if the client was unhappy for *any* reason. This sounds good in theory, but one issue with these programs in practice is that they might encourage clients to focus too much on short-term performance, at the expense of longer-term results.

If you're just getting started and/or if your portfolio is small and might stay that way for a while because your disposable in-come is limited, hiring an adviser who is truly fee-only might not be a viable option. Because these advisers earn money as a percentage of your assets, many might say they work primar-ily with those who have accumulated larger portfolios so they can cover the costs of doing business. And while there are many arguments in favor of working with an adviser, implementing the Five Fundamentals is easy enough that you can certainly do so on your own. All the investment products I particularly like (except for DFA funds that are available only through qualified independent advisers) can be accessed with an account at Fidel-ity, Schwab, or many other discount brokerages, or simply by opening an account at Vanguard. If you have a smaller account but would still prefer the counsel of an adviser, consider hiring a financial planner who charges by the hour to help you develop your asset-allocation plan. Because that's the single most impor-tant part of your investment process, and also the part where professional help can be most valuable, it makes sense to seek out an adviser who is willing to take the time to understand your personal circumstances and long-term objectives, and develop the right asset allocation for you. Then you can take responsibil-ity for implementing the plan yourself and return to the adviser once a year for an annual checkup of your financial health. Just make sure if you hire a financial planner by the hour, you commit to implementing the plan she has developed on your behalf. I have seen too many people shell out good money to create a solid financial plan only to leave it lying dormant, gathering dust on the shelf instead of working hard for them to generate wealth. If you are going to pay for a financial plan, make sure you put it to good use!

For those with larger or more complex portfolios, independent fee-only advisers can earn their fees by adding value to their clients' portfolios by providing them with long-term support on a wide variety of issues. They can start by motivating you to invest your assets and developing a plan for you with a target asset allocation. They can also help you implement it and stick to it when markets are down and you're tempted to sell low. This, I have found, is one of the things my clients benefit from the most—an objective perspective and a reminder of the importance of adhering to their long-term plan.

As I've noted, you can expect to pay a typical fee-only adviser about 1 percent of the assets she manages annually. If your portfolio climbs into the millions of dollars (and let's hope it does!), that fee will start to fall in percentage terms because it will climb in absolute dollar amounts and cover the cost of the services your adviser provides. If you include all types of fees, less than 1.5 percent total in most cases is OK, 1.25 percent is good, and less than 1 percent is very good. The most important piece of advice, though, is simply to pay attention; if two products look similar, don't just pick one on a whim. Look at the fees associated with each and opt for the less expensive version.

You'll never manage to avoid paying any fees at all—and you

really don't want to. If you're not paying fees directly, it usually means someone else is doing it indirectly on your behalf, and that someone may not have your best interests as the top priority. So follow the Fifth Fundamental and keep your fees as low as possible. This may spell the difference between failure and success in reaching your long-term goals.

7

GETTING STARTED
AND STAYING
ON TRACK

with the
Five Fundamentals

You've already taken several important steps toward securing your financial future. You've abandoned—or at least started to question—the harmful mind-sets that have for so long convinced women they shouldn't care about investing their money. You've read this book and educated yourself on how investing works so you can make informed decisions and ask better questions when investing your money. You've learned the Five Fundamentals and now understand why a commonsense, simple-to-execute investment plan is the best possible strategy for building wealth, and that you're better off ignoring anyone who tells you otherwise.

Now that you have all this information at your disposal, how do you put it to work for you? How do you get started and stay on track? And then, how do you stay focused in a world and an industry where things are constantly changing and where the markets and the people commenting on them will consistently test your willpower to stick to the Five Fundamentals? In this chapter we'll explore how to do just that—helping you develop a pragmatic plan for moving forward and answering some of the most important questions you'll encounter along the way.

Where Is All Your Money?

The first step is to figure out where you currently stand financially. Where is all your money? You might think this is a dumb question. Who loses track of their money? But you'd be amazed at how few people can provide an instant, complete, and accurate answer. One survey by the Investment Company Institute found that the money-management firms that make up its membership reported tens of thousands of "abandoned" 401(k) accounts containing balances of anywhere from $2 to $74,304.[1] Employees job-hop so frequently that they forget about one plan among many, or perhaps an employer loses track of a former employee. Maybe the company now goes by a new name because it has merged or been bought by another company. Maybe it went out of business and simply doesn't exist anymore.

If you know where your old 401(k) plan accounts are, it will be easy to track down your money because you should continue to get statements in the mail or can readily look up information online. If that's the case, simply compile the most recent statement for each of your accounts and add up the amounts to find out the total you have saved in your 401(k)s.

If you don't know where those accounts are, first locate any old W-2s to make sure you made contributions to the 401(k) plans of the various companies you worked for while you were employed. If you don't have those old tax documents, the process will take a bit more time, but it can still be done. Contact your former employers, and get them to check their records to see if you or they contributed to a retirement account for you. If you can't track down your old employer for some reason, try to contact the plan administrator (such as Fidelity) to find out if you have an account with them. There's also a national registry of unclaimed retirement account plan balances provided by employers.

Next, if you have any other retirement accounts you oversee yourself, such as an IRA or Roth IRA, make a list of all of them along with your 401(k)s.

Then make a list of any taxable, non-retirement accounts, such as bank accounts (both savings and checking accounts) and brokerage accounts. Add up the value of each account to figure out the total amount of your investable assets.

Consolidate!

Once you've figured out the value of all of your investable assets, the next step is to get all these assets into as few places as possible, physically, so they are easier for you to manage. Consolidate your funds with as few custodians (i.e., firms that look after, or hold, your assets) as possible. Discount brokerages such as Fidelity, Schwab, and Vanguard don't charge separate fees for acting as your custodian because they make their money in other ways—by charging you a fee to make trades, for instance, or to park your cash in one of their money market savings accounts or purchase their proprietary products. This is good news for you because it means there's no additional cost you have to pay to consolidate and streamline your investment accounts at these brokerage firms.

I recommend using one custodian to keep things as simple as possible. Stick with one that charges low trading fees (to buy the index mutual funds and ETFs you'll be using to drive your investments) as well as an "open architecture" platform that will enable you to buy investment products from as wide an array of providers as possible (some brokerage firms will limit what you can buy). For instance, if you have an account at Fidelity, you can still purchase Vanguard funds. Also check that the assets at your custodian will be insured (just ask them), so that even if some disaster befalls that custodian, your money will be safe. If you want to hedge your bets and protect your money still further, you could split your portfolio between two custodians, but adding any more than that to the mix can make things unwieldy.

After you've selected a custodian, further consolidate your assets by putting them in as few accounts as possible. For example, if you have any old 401(k) plans, transfer them into a single IRA rollover account. If you move those funds into an IRA rollover account—which you can do without incurring any tax consequences—you'll immediately be able to access a far greater range of investment options because you will no longer be restricted to those that your employer and the plan administrator have decided to make available for the 401(k).

Assuming you currently work for a company that offers a 401(k), you'll now have two tax-sheltered retirement accounts: the rollover IRA and your current employers' 401(k). If you don't have one already, you might want to set up a third retirement account in the form of a traditional or regular IRA so you can make additional contributions without going through your employer, and take advantage of the wider array of options the IRA offers. (This is especially something to look into if your employer does not offer a retirement plan option.) If you keep your former 401(k) assets separate from regular IRA contributions, this may also give you some advantages in the future because 401(k) assets have had better protection from creditors in bankruptcy situations. If you anticipate your tax bracket will be much higher in retirement than it is now, it likely makes sense for you to open a Roth IRA account as opposed to a traditional one. A Roth IRA differs from a regular IRA in that you pay taxes on any funds you invest before you set them aside rather than when you withdraw the funds in retirement. This can work to your advantage in the long run if you end up in a higher tax bracket when you retire than you are in when you initially invest the funds, because your tax burden for the Roth IRA will be determined by your current (lower) bracket.

In general, Roth IRAs especially make sense for young people when they are just starting out, because they are likely in a lower tax bracket now than they will be later in life. Any money put in their Roth IRA now can grow tax-free for the rest of their life (and even potentially into the next generation). If you have children who earn some income and you and they can afford it, consider helping them fund Roth IRAs while they are still in very low tax brackets, such as when they have summer or part-time jobs. This will not only allow them to start reaping the benefits of the market as early as possible, it will also get them in the habit of investing so that when they have money to invest in the future, they will already be accustomed to and comfortable with the investing process.

Should I Pay Off My Debt Before I Invest?

If you have debt with high interest rates—whether it be credit card debt or student loan debt—you'll have to determine how much money to set aside toward paying that down versus how much you invest. Any debt you have ultimately offsets the value of your assets, so as important as it is to invest extra income as early as possible, you should not do so if it will undermine your ability to pay off this debt. Depending on your circumstances, it usually makes sense to focus on paying down debt before you start investing. In some cases, it might make more sense to do both at once. Regarding mortgage debt on your home, if you have a relatively low interest rate, it usually makes financial sense to have that debt and still focus on investing.

The situation will be different for everyone, but as a general rule of thumb, you should *always* take advantage of any 401(k) matches your company provides—even if you have debt. If your company says it will match, say, up to 5 percent of your salary in 401(k) contributions if you make the same 5 percent investment, make sure you do so. This money from your employer, in the form of additional funds for your 401(k), is basically free money: it's the equivalent of instantly earning a 100 percent return on your investment and then having that windfall go on to generate investment returns for you each and every year, as long as you have it working for you. When you are starting out, failing to take advantage of this match is one of the biggest mistakes you can make (along with not investing at all). Even if you later find yourself in tight financial circumstances and have to borrow against your 401(k) assets, or even pay a penalty for withdrawing money from your 401(k) plan early, you'll still be ahead of the game because you'll have captured the benefits of these employer matches.

Investing 5 percent may seem like a lot if you are just starting out or if you have a lot of debt, but another advantage of putting money toward a regular 401(k) is that anything you invest comes out of pretax dollars. Because you don't pay tax on this money until you withdraw it from the account—which likely won't be for a few decades—any dollar you invest is effectively worth more than any dollar that is taxed up front. Plus, having this money set aside before your income is taxed reduces your overall tax burden for the year. In other words, investing $100 a month toward retirement does not mean your take-home pay will be reduced by $100. Plus, because your employer withdraws the money automatically, it may feel less onerous psychologically.

The second rule of thumb related to debt is always to make the minimum payment each month on any debt you're carrying. You don't want to ruin your credit or default on a loan because you put that money toward your 401(k). The question is, should you set aside any extra income beyond this minimum to put toward retirement or to pay down your debt more quickly?

This answer will be different for everyone—because everyone's loan structure, income, interest rate, type of loan, and so on will be different—so it makes sense to speak with a financial adviser to figure out the best strategy for you. If you're self-employed, work for a company that doesn't have a 401(k) plan, or have an employer that doesn't offer to match the first 3 percent or 5 percent or so of your contributions to that 401(k) plan, you should just concentrate on paying off any credit card debt. The interest on that debt will likely accrue much more rapidly than any gains on your investments, making it that much more difficult to claw yourself out of this debt later on. When you've gotten rid of that burden, then you can turn your attention to saving and investing.

As for student loan debt, if you work in a sector that qualifies for loan forgiveness, then you're probably better off making the minimum payment and setting anything extra aside for retirement because your earnings are going to do so much more work for you in a retirement plan. Of course, many of these forgiveness plans don't kick in until you've made about ten years of payments, and they don't cover all types of loans, so you'd need to do your homework—and obviously not count your chickens before they hatch. If you do qualify, keep making the minimum payments but put any extra income toward your retirement account.

When Should I Invest?

Now! Once you have paid down your debt (or are in the process of doing so responsibly) and created an emergency fund as I discussed in chapter 3, you should focus on contributing every dollar you can to your 401(k) account or on maxing out your contributions to your other retirement accounts.

The younger you are, the more valuable those dollars are, because they'll accumulate and earn investment returns for many more years. Let's say you begin putting $4,000 a year into your retirement accounts when you are 22. By the time you are 62, the miracle of compounding (which I explained in chapter 1) will ensure that you will have a million dollars in your portfolio, if the average annual return is 8 percent. If you postpone the age at which you start contributing by just a decade, to 32, and still want to end up a millionaire, you'll have to invest more than twice as much every year to reach the same target, or almost $9,000 a year. That's how much difference those early years will make to you. Postponing your decision to invest from your thirties until your forties will make a big difference too, and so on. Of course, that doesn't mean that if you've hit 50 and still haven't done anything, you should simply throw your arms up in the air and decide there's no point. This is just a message to those in their twenties that the wind is in their favor: they don't have to save nearly as much, in dollar terms, to end up in the same place. (If you're looking for help or insight, the Securities and Exchange Commission offers a great compound interest calculator at investor.gov to show you precisely what happens in different scenarios.)

When you're investing new cash in the market, the best strategy is usually to put it all to work at once because, as I discussed in chapter 2, the odds are likely that stocks will go up rather than down over the long run. Still, psychologically it is hard for many people to do this because they worry the market will go down right after they invest. If you feel this way, you can opt to practice what is known as dollar cost averaging. It sounds like a fancy term, but all it means is that you divide the amount you want to invest into smaller amounts (I call them "tranches") and buy gradually on a regular schedule you set for yourself. That way, if the market goes down after you invest the first tranche, you'll still have more tranches of funds to invest and can buy in at the now-lower price. And if the market goes up after you invest the first tranche, you'll be happy you started investing when you did. This is the approach I take when I have to invest a large amount of new money for a nervous client, and if dollar cost averaging is what it takes to give you the confidence to put your money to work, use it!

Consider Tax Consequences

If you have both taxable accounts and retirement accounts, you should consider how allocating funds to each of these will affect how much you owe in taxes over the long haul. After all, this book is about maximizing your future potential wealth, so in addition to staying true to the Five Fundamentals, you should take advantage of strategies when investing that will help you reduce your lifetime tax burden.

Because you pay taxes on any income and capital gains you earn in non-retirement accounts on an annual basis, you can dip into taxable accounts at any time and for whatever reason, and the only tax you'll pay will be on any taxable gains you realized (triggered) by selling off your shares (unless you can offset those gains through tax-loss harvesting as discussed in chapter 5). In contrast, there are limits on how much you can access the assets in your retirement accounts before you reach retirement age without having to pay big penalties and taxes on the withdrawals.

In general, I try to put investments that generate a lot of income in retirement accounts so that income won't be taxed each year. So for example, I am more likely to put large company value index funds in retirement accounts because the value funds are likely to generate more dividends than other index funds. The same is true for those investments that will generate a lot of capital gains, such as mutual funds that will have a relatively high rate of internal turnover, i.e., small company index funds. In contrast I'm more likely to use ETFs, such as an S&P 500 ETF, in taxable accounts, because they are less likely to generate taxable capital gains as long as I don't sell my holdings.

One important thing to remember is to try to avoid overloading your taxable account(s) with too many risky assets if you know you will need that money relatively soon (within the next five to ten years, say). Also, you should put any municipal bond investments in your taxable account because they will be free of federal—and perhaps even state—tax.

While we're on the subject of taxes, you also need to consider what the tax consequences will be of selling any of the assets in those accounts. If you are rebalancing your portfolio or decide to fund the down payment on your house, or any other big purchase, by liquidating some of your non-retirement portfolio, you need to be strategic. What are the consequences of using this money now and having to pay the capital gains taxes as a result?

If the investment has appreciated a lot—imagine someone who bought the S&P 500 at the bottom of the recent financial crisis and has since more than doubled her money, for instance—you'll end up paying a hefty tax bill because it has appreciated in value so much. You may decide to take the tax hit today and just move on with your life. Alternatively, you could sell something else that isn't doing so well and that won't leave you with a tax obligation. If you do this, you can hold on to those investments with the big returns and worry about the tax burden later. Assuming you otherwise have enough money invested to live on and you have plans to donate to charity, you could even donate these investments directly to charity later on as a way to avoid paying the capital gains tax. Donating appreciated stock not only saves you the tax hit and allows you to contribute to a worthy cause, it also gets you the full tax credit that comes with any charitable donation. It's a tax win-win.

Another thing to consider is that if, upon your death, you have appreciated investments in taxable accounts, current laws entitle your heirs to a "step up in basis," which means they will not have to pay the capital gains tax on those appreciated investments. In this way, you not only avoid the tax consequences for yourself, you also pass on what could be a significant tax break to your family.

When thinking about saving money on taxes, though, be careful to ensure you don't let the tax considerations lead you to having a portfolio that is too out of balance with your target asset allocation. That would be having the tax tail wag the dog.

If I Want to Hire an Adviser, What Questions Should I Ask?

Working with an adviser offers many advantages. Among other things, you pay for level-headed advice in times of market turmoil, when your emotions otherwise might overcome your common sense and lead you astray, wreaking havoc on your portfolio. He or she will also take care of all the tasks that need to be done that you might postpone or avoid because they feel too complex or too time-consuming. How do I pick the right funds? How do I rebalance? No problem; your adviser will handle that task for you.

If you do want to work with an adviser, there are some important questions you should ask of anyone you're considering. The first one is whether she subscribes to the tenets of the Five Fundamentals. Will she help you build a diversified portfolio of low-cost index funds, and rebalance that to maintain the correct long-term asset allocation? If not, even if you find an adviser you like and feel you can trust, the two of you won't be on the same page philosophically, and you'll be setting yourself up for problems down the road.

The second crucial question is whether, as we discussed in the previous chapter, she is a fee-only adviser and therefore required to uphold the fiduciary standard and always act in your best interests before her own. If the adviser can't clearly state this is the case, chances are she earns at least some of her money on commission, which means she has an incentive to sell you products you either don't need or that aren't as beneficial to your long-term goals. If you find this to be the case, run!

There are some other, more basic questions any adviser should be happy to answer for you before you decide whether or not to work with them. One of these is who is going to be the custodian of the investments? There is no reason for your financial adviser to have custody of your portfolio, and a separate custodian will ensure your money is safe and the statements you are receiving are accurate. This provides you with checks and balances, the most basic of which is the ability to check one statement against the other and ensure that they match. My clients receive statements from me as well as statements from the discount or retail brokerage firm I use as a custodian, which means they can check one against the other to verify they are accurate. Why is this so important? Well, when Bernie Madoff's clients signed on with him, they probably didn't realize—or didn't care—that the custodian of their assets was an affiliate of Madoff's own firm. This should have served as a big red flag. Madoff's Ponzi scheme could never have worked as it did had he used an independent custodian, because the fraudulent statements he was producing for his clients wouldn't have matched those from an independent third party.

You should also ask your adviser about what he includes (or doesn't include) in the portfolio, and how he structures it. Obviously, because you'll want to be sure you're adhering to the Five Fundamentals, you'll want to know what asset-allocation model they use for your portfolio. What specific investments have they selected, and why? For example, do they use index funds? How are the various investment classes weighted within your portfolio?

Which market benchmark does your potential adviser think is the best comparison for your portfolio—and why—when it comes to judging how well you're doing? What are the tax consequences of all the decisions she would make in managing the portfolio?

If you pick up any signs that the adviser you're thinking of working with is uncomfortable with those questions, or being less than forthcoming with the answers, the best thing you can do is walk away.

Should I Use the New Adviser Alternatives?

Robo Advisers

A new low-cost way to have your money managed is by investing with so-called robo advisers. These are automated online investment-management systems that use computer algorithms to do everything from calculating what they believe to be your optimal asset allocation to selecting an investment portfolio and undertaking routine tasks such as rebalancing. Robo advisers use their automated investing tools to relieve you of most of the tasks that can overwhelm you and stop you from acting. All you have to do is make the initial decisions: pick one, fill out an on-line questionnaire, and hand over the money to invest. A couple of early movers in this space that you may have heard of include Betterment and Wealthfront. Bigger players have also gotten in, including Charles Schwab, Fidelity, and Vanguard. There is even one focused on women called Ellevest.

If a robo adviser will help you get moving on your investments, then it could be useful for you to use one, but there are a few things to consider before you sign on. Each of these firms has its own assumptions about which asset-allocation model is optimal, and it takes some digging to figure out what that is. Yes, most robo advisers offer low fees, and yes, they almost always implement their recommended asset allocation using index funds. Those are, indeed, two of the Five Fundamentals. But don't forget that by far the most important of the fundamentals when it comes to generating returns is the nature of your asset allocation. That is what is going to determine your results. If you turn this responsibility over to a robo adviser, you'll have to compare their asset allocations and assess what they overweight and what they underweight, relative to the whole world of publicly traded stocks and to your own target asset allocation. (Therefore, ideally, you should already have developed your own target asset allocation, either independently or with the help of a financial adviser.) If you can't find a robo adviser with an asset-allocation model that is transparent and that basically matches your target allocation, you're better off doing it yourself. Sure, it means you'll have to take responsibility for handling tasks such as portfolio rebalancing, but even if it feels daunting the first time you do it, you'll quickly realize it is actually pretty simple, and you will become more comfortable with it over time.

Target-Date Funds

If you want another relatively low-cost option for managing your funds for retirement, you can consider target-date funds. These are mutual funds that choose your asset allocation for you based on when you want to retire. As you approach retirement, the fund automatically adjusts that asset allocation to make it more conservative. These can be a good solution if you want to make one decision now (when you want to retire), or if you don't have a lot of money to invest in a diversified portfolio of index funds yourself. But as with choosing a robo adviser, you need to make sure you know what the underlying asset allocation is and that it's right for you. Everyone has a different risk tolerance. So even if you are planning to retire in twenty-five years, for example, you may want to choose a target-date fund that is longer or shorter than that depending on the asset allocation you want. Then over time you should look at how the asset allocation in the fund changes and ensure it is still aligned with the asset allocation that makes sense for your particular situation and risk tolerance. For example, as you get closer to your supposed retirement date, you may change your mind about when you are going to retire, or perhaps you may decide you want to work part-time and therefore can delay the date at which you need to start drawing on your retirement accounts. This will all influence how aggressive your asset allocation should be, and it may not match the asset allocation of the fund you have chosen.

Also, make sure the underlying funds the target-date fund uses are low-fee index funds and that the fee for the target-date fund itself is low. Otherwise you could be paying two layers of relatively high fees.

Investment Circles Can Help

Regardless of whether you hire an adviser, use a robo adviser or a target date fund, or just invest yourself, some women advocate joining investment circles as a way to boost financial confidence and overcome the paralysis that can afflict them when it comes to getting more engaged with their investing. One such group I've encountered was Directions for Women, founded in 2009 by Eleanor Blayney, Peg Downey, and Elizabeth Jetton. The company has now taken another form: Elizabeth Jetton trains local financial advisers to host and oversee Money Circle gatherings, or group discussions for both existing and potential clients, on a community-by-community basis. The goal is to provide a "safe, collaborative atmosphere for women to begin talking about a topic not usually discussed in 'polite' conversation." It's not so much that the atmosphere suddenly becomes raucous; rather, the women lose their inhibitions about raising questions they've always had about money but have never felt comfortable asking anyone before. Directions for Women found that 71 percent of attendees polled reported, with relief, "I am not alone in my struggles."

One of the reasons I formed PowerHouse Assets was to address this feeling so many women have and then, importantly, move it from awareness to action. At our two-hour educational gatherings, attendees discuss the Five Fundamentals and talk as openly with each other as they want to (and usually the women are pretty open) about their questions, confusion, fears, etc. regarding money and investing. I make a point of starting each gathering by stating that, especially in this context, there is no such thing as a stupid question. I also ask the group to agree that, to the extent women discuss their personal situations during these gatherings, we keep the conversation confidential after we leave. PowerHouse attendees have included Wall Street veterans as well as women who arrived not knowing what a stock was, much less how it differed from a bond. We pooled our knowledge and helped each other learn, ensuring everyone emerged from these intimate gatherings (held in the homes of friends or acquaintances) with a much deeper understanding of the fundamentals of investing and a strong resolve to invest and to stop being on the sidelines of their own financial well-being and future. Together we can help each other move forward and avoid falling into traps.

Don't Get Distracted by Unnecessary Products

Now that you have a game plan, you're ready to dive in and put your money to work. However, as is so often the case, it may be easier to stay focused on the Five Fundamental Rules in theory than in practice. Many of the money issues I discussed in the introduction—the idea that women aren't good with money or that it's selfish to care about money—may continue to distract you, holding you back from taking full advantage of the wisdom offered by the Five Fundamentals. It doesn't help, either, that Wall Street has caught on to the fact that women control trillions of dollars of wealth but that they too often refrain from taking full ownership of that money by investing it. Wall Street seeks to profit from women's psychological barriers and reluctance to "own" their money, developing new products and even entirely new investment businesses designed expressly to entice women to become investors.

So what's the problem with that? Haven't I been advocating for a more woman-friendly investment industry, one that treats us as equals? Well, yes—but only partly. If Wall Street consistently urged women to invest in a responsible, disciplined, low-cost way, then I'd be breaking out the champagne. Unfortunately, so much of what counts as "new" on Wall Street is simply a tool designed to make professional investors and wealth managers more money. And too often they prey on stereotypes about women and money rather than actually considering the futures of those women.

One of the ways they do this is by playing on our sense of altruism. A survey by Barclays Wealth found women not only donate twice as much to philanthropic causes as men, but they also appear to be more interested in finding a way to align their investment activities with their social, cultural, economic, environmental, and religious values, and with their other community engagements.[2] This has contributed to the movement known as impact investing, a form of investing designed not only to generate financial returns but also to promote a larger, more positive impact on the world. The impact investing philosophy asks, "Why not make money while simultaneously making the world a better place?"

Wanting to do good in the world is great motivation, and if you're fortunate to have enough extra income that you can save for the future, then it's only natural that you should feel a desire to give back in some way. And if you come to investing with firmly held convictions on certain social or political issues that already define your way of life and you clearly understand and accept the trade-offs, then this section likely will not apply to you because you'll want your beliefs to be reflected in your investment portfolio, just as they are in every other facet of your life. But in the case of most investors, I want to caution you against buying an investment product simply because it markets itself as aligning with your values. More often than not, and for a variety of reasons, these are not the best picks for your long-term financial well-being.

Investment strategies for investing in publicly traded stocks that emphasize having a transformative impact on the world, by definition, don't put a priority on ensuring you have the right asset allocation or the lowest-cost investment products. That means that over the course of several decades, you could forfeit tens of thousands of dollars—or much more, depending on the size of your portfolio—in potential earnings. Those are profits you might have needed to ensure your own financial security (so that you don't become one of those problems for society that you tried to solve via your investments). Or they might be excess profits that you could have funneled directly to the cause of your choice, giving those very targeted organizations or companies more direct resources to address the causes close to your heart (more than they would have received through a general publicly traded impact investment fund).

There are a few reasons many values-based investment products tend to underperform as compared to more straightforward, index-based investments. First, because they are designed to promote certain causes, they end up with a big, overweight position in certain industries and/or screening out entire sectors that are not in line with their mission. When you invest in this way, you are betting on some sectors of the economy to do better over time than others, which, as we saw in our discussion of rebalancing, is not a safe bet.

Some try to avoid this trap by choosing to invest in companies that uphold the best ethical or environmental standards as compared to their peers in that particular industry or sector. (Dimensional Fund Advisors, whose funds I use with my clients, takes this approach with their Sustainability Investing.) This tactic is better in that it doesn't leave the fund with a bias either for or against an entire sector, but because the managers define the "best" companies based on what their particular values screens tell them, they end up creating a different kind of distortion. You may end up with a portfolio that is balanced between sectors but whose individual stocks are chosen based on noneconomic considerations as opposed to their optimal blend of growth prospects and value pricing. The stocks you own could be relatively expensive or have other issues that make them less than optimal as investments. (DFA tries to overcome this by first selecting stocks that have higher expected returns based on size and value screens, and then looking for companies with sustainable or social values.) Worst of all, you have been distracted from the very straightforward approach to investing—one that is easy to understand, to learn, and to implement—that I explained in the Five Fundamentals.

Some values-based investment products can do as well, or nearly as well, as the S&P 500 over some periods of time, though they are still problematic. For instance, the Amana Mutual Funds

Trust Growth Fund Investor, which invests according to Islamic principles, has beaten the S&P 500 over the ten- and fifteen-year periods (although it fell short of the S&P 500's returns in the three- and five-year time periods). But if you did buy this fund, you'd own no banking stocks, stakes in other financial firms, or even real estate positions, because Islam prohibits charging interest. That's a whole swathe of the economy that will almost certainly do well at some point, meaning owners of this fund will miss out on any of these potential future returns. Meanwhile, the fund's fees are more than 1 percent per year. You can see similar patterns in a number of socially responsible or impact funds. Several of them have produced competitive returns, but when they do, it usually is the result of portfolios that are skewed in favor of certain sectors of the economy. That means you are actively betting that those sectors will continue to outperform—a strategy that, as I've already demonstrated, is seriously flawed.

And even if you want to hold yourself to a specific standard when investing in the stock markets, it isn't always so easy to do. Let's assume, for example, that you want to remove exposure to fossil fuels from your portfolio, an increasingly common desire today. It's simple to know where to start: by cutting the stocks of oil exploration and development companies from your holdings. Some individuals then go on to remove automakers as well, or utilities that also rely on fossil fuels to generate power. But what about food processors? They are one of the heaviest users of fossil fuels, both in their manufacturing operations and in their transport of goods to retail outlets. Or retailers themselves? Many import products for sale from China, whose environmental records are appalling, and consume tremendous resources while transporting them. Some money-management firms, such as Domini Social Investments, will assemble portfolios that actively select companies that do no harm, but their equity funds also carry above-average fees of about 1.2 to 1.6 percent (compared to less than 0.10 percent for a typical S&P 500 index fund). You're paying a steep premium for that "fossil-free fund," *and* you'll end up with the same distorted portfolio.

One investment category that may seem like a good bet—especially given the themes of this book—comprises those that are targeted directly toward women. But investing is gender-neutral, which means there is no need to buy a special product, especially because anything that is custom-designed to appeal to a particular segment of the market will likely be more expensive because it is more complicated to manage.

The Pax Ellevate Global Women's Index Fund is a double whammy: it's marketed primarily to women and is also an impact product because it invests only in women-led companies or companies with lots of women on their boards. I strongly believe in promoting female leadership in management and on boards. Unfortunately, at the time of this writing, the fund has a fee of 0.74 percent—less than many actively managed mutual funds but more than fourteen times what you'd pay to invest in the Standard & Poor's 500 index fund (which also would give you more balanced exposure to the stock market). I'm not saying don't invest in this. Nor am I saying it won't have good returns—it may. But you're paying for the privilege of investing with your principles rather than the Five Fundamentals, and you're at risk if the market doesn't favor your values.

The Pax Ellevate Global Women's Index Fund includes holdings such as PepsiCo (whose CEO, Indra Nooyi, is a woman) and Lockheed Martin (where a third of the board members are women). The fund's ability to outperform a global bench-mark hinges on whether the strongest-performing sectors in the global markets will be those that have women in leadership positions—and whether these women remain in those positions. Nooyi will eventually leave PepsiCo as CEO, and if the succeed-ing CEO happens to be a man, and the company continues to do well, any investors in the Pax fund may lose out on those gains if PepsiCo is not included in the fund simply because it no longer meets the gender criteria.

The point is that, even if you are passionately committed to a particular cause, there are other, more effective ways to sup-port it that don't compromise your long-term investment goals. You can, as mentioned earlier, donate some of the profits you make from your investments to charity—or even donate the appreciated assets themselves directly to an organization you support. If you save and invest enough money, you could afford to change careers or go back to school or run for office so you could pass legislation that supports the causes you hold dear. You could fund a grant program or scholarship fund that pro-vides money directly to people who are doing important work, or provide some capital to venture funds or start-up companies focused on new services or products you believe in. So many possibilities open up to you when you have financial resources at your disposal. Why sacrifice that for an expensive investment product for the stock markets that may not focus as directly on what you want to support?

I also want to take a moment to point out that simply by putting your money to work in the stock market, you *are* doing good. Not only are you on track to support yourself and your family—an extremely worthy cause—and do what you can to close the gender investment gap, but you're also supporting the economy as a whole. By investing your money in the companies in the index funds, you are allowing those companies to put it to work coming up with new innovations and creating jobs in their communities.

In recent years, the "sharing economy" has caught on, with people sharing their cars, vacation homes, etc. It makes everyone feel good that these things are being shared and put to good use, rather than just sitting idle when the owner doesn't use them. Your savings aren't exactly the same as an unused vacation home or car. But if you don't invest that capital and put it to work, it's being underused. So why not invest, putting your money to work in something? You'll be funneling your money into the economy and supporting job growth. You'll enable entrepreneurs to expand and innovate.

Moreover, there is nothing selfish or unethical about ensuring you have enough resources for your life, and that your family is taken care of. Taking care of future generations will prevent your children and grandchildren from becoming dependent on society, meaning that whatever safety net or charitable resources are available can be put to use serving those who are truly in need. Plus it allows your descendants to make choices about their lives and careers without having to focus as much on financial concerns. Maybe your granddaughter will be able to engage in lower-paying work she truly loves—such as becoming a teacher or an artist—or become an entrepreneur because she doesn't need to fret as much about taking on that financial risk. Now that's an impact you can be proud of too.

Sit Back and Relax

Once you've followed these steps, congratulate yourself! You have overcome your fears and conquered your procrastination, taken control of your financial destiny, and taken the first steps toward ensuring you will be in a position to take full advantage of all the opportunities and choices life brings your way, and not have to turn them down because you haven't been prudent with your money. As long as you move forward following the Five Fundamentals, then all you need to do for your investing now is relax.

Open that bottle of champagne and toast yourself. Your money is now working for you, just as it should. You can now go off and pursue your other goals, whatever they may be, and enjoy the rest of the riches in your life.

A FINANCIAL
FUTURE
SO BRIGHT
YOU CAN
PAY IT FORWARD

Now that you have reached the end of this book, I hope you feel as though we have been on a journey together. At the beginning of this journey, perhaps you didn't know where to start to set about becoming more engaged in your own finances, while the very idea of beginning a systematic investment program may well have felt overwhelming. For other reasons—the majority of them being the myths I discussed and then shattered for you in the introductory chapters—you may not even have been convinced at the outset that this was a journey on which you wanted to embark. You might have succumbed to the propaganda that investing is all just too complicated or that caring about money makes you greedy or that investing is something only the wealthiest among us need to pay attention to.

Now, having followed the evidence I've assembled for you, you know that none of that is true. Investing doesn't have to be complicated, and anyone—regardless of income level or previous experience in the markets—can succeed at it. In fact, the more complicated you find your investing strategy to be and the more you try to capture short-term gains by timing the market, the more likely you are actually to *lose* money in the long run.

At the same time, loving money does not make you selfish or shallow but quite the opposite. Loving money simply means you love the idea of financial independence and freedom to choose the life you want to live. It means you love your life and want to make the most of it rather than remain a wallflower always asking, "What if?"

Moreover, loving money means that no matter how easy it is to make excuses—"I'm too busy," "It's boring," "I'm terrible at math," or "My husband takes care of all that for me"—investing and knowing how to properly manage or oversee the management of those investments is vital for your future and that of your family. Loving money is about loving yourself and respecting the hard work you (or your family members, if you've inherited money) have put into earning money in the first place—going to college, working hard at your career, and saving and spending responsibly—so all that effort is not for naught.

I spend each and every day of my professional life trying to find ways to help my clients understand all this, and then to help them take the tangible steps that will bring them closer to reaching their financial goals. Even when I'm not working on their portfolios, or talking with them, somewhere in the back of my mind, I'm thinking about their very specific issues—and also about the bigger ones I have addressed in this book: *How*

*can I introduce some rationality into the overwhelming and unnec-
essarily complex world of investing? How can I help my clients reach
whatever goals they have for themselves? How can I keep them from
panicking in the face of volatility to ensure they stay on track and
don't miss out on the potential future upside?*

I wrote this book so I could help you do the same thing.
Now that we've come to the end of our journey together, I hope
I have succeeded in inspiring you to take the next steps toward
protecting—and growing—your hard-earned assets. But I also
hope you won't stop there. I hope that by being a great individual investor, you will serve as an example for those around you
and thereby help close the investment gap that has kept women
on the sidelines for too long. With your knowledge of investing,
you can choose your path from here, because successful investing will give you choices and opportunities for your life. And I
hope you will encourage other women to get on the investment
path so they too will have choices and opportunities later in life.

A New Mind-Set Creates a New Path Forward

Women have always understood that money equals independence, even if we haven't always taken the next logical step by embracing an identity as investors. Too often this hesitation stems
from what we're taught—by society and the investment industry, yes, but also by those closest to us. Think about it: where
did you first learn about money? It was probably at home by
observing your parents and the way they managed it. Did your
parents openly discuss money with each other and in front of
you, or did they think it improper? Were they good savers and
investors, or were they irresponsible? Were they always stressed

about money, or were they comfortable financially? Did they share responsibilities for budgeting and investing? Did they both work, or was one considered the breadwinner? What about their friends? How do all these factors compare with the way you view money now?

I just have to look back at my own childhood and young adulthood to realize that—like many of us—I learned important money lessons from my parents. In my case, it was from my father, whose mantra was, "It's not what you make but what you save." Ironically, the most important lesson he ended up teaching me was even more powerful than his lessons on saving, even though he never actually put it into a clever catchphrase. Instead, he practiced it firsthand, and I learned by observing him. Investing, he showed me through his actions, was the real secret to building wealth.

My father was an entrepreneur (he started an importing business, mostly from Asia), but he was also a passionate investor. That was an avocation of his—and I watched him engage in it since my childhood. Observing him, I came to realize that saving was only the first step: saving gave him a pool of money he could invest in the stock market. But it was those stock investments, rather than the earnings from his business, that eventually financed my parents' lifestyle. My father was able to return to graduate school in his late forties to study Mandarin Chinese and get a master's degree in international affairs from the Fletcher School of Law and Diplomacy at Tufts University because profits from his investments enabled him to finance his studies. Later, he and my mother spent winters in Puerto Rico, in a beautiful home overlooking the ocean, where they made many wonderful new friends. This was possible because my father was a die-hard investor; it was part of his identity.

It was also possible because my father viewed money the same way most men do—as a river, not a lake. As I explained in the introduction, when we view money as a river, we recognize that it doesn't have to be a finite resource, that it can continually replenish itself through the power of investing. This mentality changes how we approach our spending and saving decisions: if we think money is a finite resource, we start to grow anxious when we see it diminish—when we're faced with a large expense or when we lose our jobs, for instance. But if we think of it as fungible and fluid, we learn to calm down because we know that, through our investment sources, our money is constantly replenishing itself. If you currently think of money as a lake, the surest way to switch your mind-set is to start investing. Once you start seeing your money grow over time, your perspective will change and you'll watch that lake transform into a beautiful flowing river.

Throughout this book, I have emphasized the importance of investing and growing your money over the long haul—keeping it working for you for years or decades until you're ready to retire. And even though, yes, you should hold off on withdrawing most of your investments for as long as possible, the great thing about this river of invested money is that, if you need it before then—for a major purchase or to start a business or go back to school like my father did—it will be there. As a very general rule, if your money is properly invested, you should be able to take out about 3.5 to 4 percent a year if you want to maintain the value of your assets after inflation. (If you want your assets to grow in real terms, then you can't take out that much.)

I started PowerHouse Assets because I love investing and find financial planning to be a rewarding career. I love helping one of my clients go from viewing money as a lake to viewing it as a river, and realize that loving money does not make you greedy but instead makes you smart and resilient and able to take charge of your life. But I also realize my capacity to do so is limited—I can't take on enough women as clients to make a dent in what I see as the need for education. Even if I quit advising and went on a tour during which I spoke to women about the Five Fundamentals, I know I'd barely be able to have an impact on the investment gap women face. That is one of the reasons I wrote this book—to share my ideas with as many people as possible so they can appreciate that investing does not have to be daunting or difficult, nor is it something only men can be good at. I hope that, now that we've reached the end of the book, you feel this way, and even if you don't quite feel like a financial expert, you're at least inspired to learn what you can.

My vision for you is that, using your newfound knowledge, you will create a new world for yourself, one in which money and investing no longer make you feel anxious but instead give you confidence to pursue the life you want. I want you to feel confident in your ability to plan for your future because you understand how to look at an idea or an investment product and determine instantly whether it's worth spending another minute of your limited time contemplating, or if you can simply discard it because it doesn't fit into your carefully considered, straightforward investment strategy. I want you never again to feel paralyzed or overwhelmed when confronted with a financial or investment decision because you know most of that baffling jargon about money that you hear all around you is simply irrelevant.

In this new world, random money issues won't rattle you and

distract you nearly as much. Instead, because you have become an investor, you'll come to think of money itself in an entirely different way. It's a tool, and a means to an end—and it's also something to embrace, for that very reason. You can feel comfortable dipping into this steady stream of money in order to live the life you want, whether that's taking a dream vacation, pursuing an educational or career opportunity, being able to help out family members with education expenses or other needs, or helping a nonprofit or business venture get off the ground. You aren't just relying on what you can scrape together from your employment earnings or from stagnant savings you feel like you need to protect, but also on your investment income. Doesn't that sound appealing?

Adopting this new mind-set will not only improve your financial situation, it will pay off in other ways as well. For one, it will allow you to become a true equal in financial matters with your life partner. It's hard to overestimate the transformative impact on your relationships of becoming more confident and engaged in your financial future, especially if you're married to a man who, up until now, has been shouldering the burden of your family's financial decisions entirely on his own. Now that you understand the fundamental rules of investing, he'll be able to talk through questions about the family investments with you and share the responsibility with you today. Of course this applies to all relationships in which you share finances with another person, including if you're part of a same-sex couple or living with, but not married to, your significant other. When you talk about the future, your partner can take comfort in the awareness that, should anything happen, you'll be secure—not only in terms of your access to the wealth you've accumulated together but in your ability to manage or oversee its management on your own. If there is a medical crisis or some other emergency, you can both focus on the medical issues and on caring for each other rather than worrying about how you're going to learn to manage the family finances without the help of your life partner.

By writing this book, I hope to contribute to a change in women's mind-set with respect to money and investing. I believe the time is right. Increasingly, other women are working toward the same goal in business, and specifically within the financial industry. Perhaps few of these professional women recognize more clearly the need to undertake such changes than Andrea Jung, who became chairman and CEO of Avon Products in 1999 and took this mission with her to her next job, as president and CEO of Grameen America, the grassroots micro-lending nonprofit founded by Muhammad Yunus, which she joined in 2014. At Grameen, her task is to improve access to capital for low-income women, making small loans that will help them transform their financial and life prospects. "I am absolutely stunned, shocked at the financial inequality," she says. "Part is education, part is access [to the financial system]. If women aren't given the tools and not allowed to make their own decisions, I don't see progress."

Thanks to her work at both Avon and Grameen, Jung has become aware of just what is at stake. She has witnessed the confidence gap among potential borrowers with whom her nonprofit works, and says it manifests itself through lower business-loan approval rates by bankers when approached by women with business plans. "Men will just say, 'I'm going to go in there and get that loan,' whereas women think to themselves, *They won't give me that loan.*" At the same time, she is trying to get the financial services industry to focus on serving women's real interests. And, Jung notes, women "can't break through until we break through in financial services."

Women in my corner of the financial services industry are working toward creating more role models in our field as well. For example, the Certified Financial Planner (CFP) Board of Standards, a nonprofit organization that represents financial planners such as myself, and that establishes ethical standards for our industry, is trying to boost the number of women in the profession. While the CFP board has seen the number of financial planners grow at an impressive clip, the proportion who are women has remained largely unchanged for at least a decade, at 23 percent. To confront this, the CFP board launched its Women's Initiative, or WIN, in 2013, with the mission of figuring out why relatively few women choose to join the financial planning profession and to try to rectify the situation in order to end what it calls the industry's "feminine famine."

In addition to trying to recruit more women to the profession, many independent, fee-only financial advisers like me are trying to motivate more women to get more engaged in their own financial futures. For example, Dimensional Fund Advisors (whose index asset class funds I have used since 1994) has formed Women's Wealth Initiatives; this group of female financial advisers now meets regularly to share ideas about how best to work with their female clients so they are motivated to invest effectively for the future. The members of this group are dynamic, smart, and empathetic women, working to change the industry from within and seeking to ensure it functions better for women clients. It is inspiring to get together with these women who share my mind-set, goals, and visions.

But you don't have to work in finance in order to change the conversation about women and money. You will be a great role model for others when you take the actions described in this book. You will become a role model for your children and other children too (e.g., nieces and nephews and friends' children)— someone they can look up to as an independent woman capable of managing her finances. This goes for children of any gender. Some older adult men might still consider it unfeminine for women to know so much about money (as regrettable as this is), but to a young boy whose mother can talk about money and investing intelligently (especially when other mothers can't), this quality might become something he admires.

When my son was in his early teens, he begged me to give him "stock lessons," and he was proud when I gave a seminar about investing at his school. Recently, he joined the investing club at his high school, and we both lamented the fact that of the sixteen members, none are girls. I was glad he noticed this is an important issue, and we even discussed how it related to the subject of this book, which I was writing at the time. I asked him why he thought the club had only boys in it. He said he thought the boys liked the image of being investors but the girls didn't. At which point we both agreed that hopefully this book will help correct that.

My daughter, meanwhile, who is currently in college, appreciates that I was able to help her set up her Roth IRA using some of the money she'd earned working summer jobs. While she makes all the final investment decisions for her Roth IRA, we can discuss what her asset allocation should be and then which index funds she should invest in. She has already experienced some of the ups and downs of the stock markets, including seeing how different asset classes have different returns at different times. All this will be great experience for her when it comes time to oversee a larger portfolio in the future—and perhaps, one day, help her own children do the same.

Being a role model doesn't have to stop with being a role model for children. There are plenty of often overlooked opportunities to help women like you get started with their portfolios. Pass this book on to the other women in your life—especially young women—and talk to them about what you've learned through your own experiences with investing. Many people still operate under the assumption that it's improper—or even unladylike (whatever that means)—to discuss money in public. But learning how to be financially independent should not be a secret kept only by the 1 percent, nor should it be a practice you engage in under the dark cover of night or alone in your room with the curtains drawn. If you worry you may come off as brash or shallow by talking openly about money, think back to when you were trying to figure all this out. How often were you plagued by anxiety about the future—worried you wouldn't have enough saved up or wondering if you'd ever be able to afford your dream life? Before you picked up this book, how embarrassed or powerless did you feel when thinking about your own investing, looking at your own investment statements from your retirement account or otherwise, or when you read or heard an investment term you didn't understand? How confused were you when looking at the options available to you in your 401(k) and not knowing how to choose among them and in what proportion?

Now imagine how you would have felt if one of your friends had mentioned they'd set up their own investment portfolio and were excited by the current and/or future potential returns? Would you have sneered at them, or would you have been impressed? My guess is you would have been both impressed and relieved at finally having the chance to talk to someone you trusted about an issue that was so seemingly beyond your grasp and yet, as you knew deep down, vital to your well-being.

Now put yourself in the shoes of another woman searching for answers to her financial future. Imagine how she might feel to know she has someone she trusts with whom she can discuss these issues. I've already demonstrated what a difference you can make to your own financial future by learning to invest wisely. Imagine being able to do the same for someone else by serving as an example, answering her questions openly, or even sitting down with her to talk about her goals.

In a perfect world, this attitude would go mainstream, and all of us—men and women—would feel comfortable discussing money and investing and feel empowered by our decision to employ sane, commonsense strategies toward building our wealth. In my more whimsical moments, I sometimes imagine a kind of calming antidote to the mainstream financial media, a TV channel devoted to the Five Fundamentals designed to help ordinary investors—mostly women—succeed in this manner. It would end up being a rather relaxing channel—more PBS than CNBC. The anchors could talk about long-term market trends, but they'd do so in a way that was level-headed and patient. Their goal would not be to get you to keep watching by inciting panic and making you believe the only way to survive is to listen to their "expert" advice. Instead, their goal would be to inform, to give viewers only the information they need to make the wisest long-term investment decisions while ignoring the fast talking or even shouting going on elsewhere. The anchors and guests would screen out any market hullaballoo that doesn't relate to implementing the Five Fundamentals, and there would be lots of time to talk about interesting subjects, even those that aren't related to investing, because the anchors and guests wouldn't have to waste time with hedge fund managers debating whether the market will go up or down in the next day, week, or month, or delving into the details of individual stocks.

Maybe it could showcase what investing has enabled women to do with their lives. It could tell the world the story of a woman who just founded an artisanal bakery, a travel firm, or a technology company with her investment earnings. Or it could feature someone who tapped her investment portfolio to help family members with education expenses so they wouldn't have staggering debt when they graduated, or financed a family reunion, bringing together three or four generations at a vacation resort in the Rockies at her expense for a week of festivities.

If television audiences required some kind of drama in order to stay interested, the channel could develop a show in which women compete to see how quickly and effectively they can locate their assets and invest them according to a solid allocation model and investment plan that follows the Five Fundamentals. The woman who has done the best job at getting her previously disorganized finances organized and working for her in the fastest way possible would be rewarded with cheers from the audience. And of course there would be plenty of prizes for the runners-up who all followed the same path.

In a nutshell, the show would feature women supporting each other in the world of investing, ensuring money never again makes them—or the audience—feel isolated, confused, or even fearful. They could talk about what's happening in the world, in their local communities, or in their lives. Occasionally—maybe once a quarter—the anchors would summarize how various investment asset classes have performed, and explain what factors lay behind those returns. But mostly it would show how women put their money to work and how they then get on with the business of simply living, while the market does its thing, making money in the long run.

Because that's precisely the future I want for you—a future surrounded by the people and pursuits that give your life meaning, while your money is working for you. I hope that by reading this book you have come to realize you can make sure your money is working for you efficiently, shrug off the myths that have shrouded women and money for too long, and emerge as a financially confident woman. I hope you can follow the simple steps I have laid out in the pages of this book, and now possess a clearer understanding of how markets work and how to make them work *for you*. And ultimately, I hope you will be able to put your own plan into operation, that you will be able to say to your friends, "Yes, my money is working for me over in my investment portfolio. It's helping me to build wealth that will provide me with the choices and opportunities I want for the future. It's doing all this while I focus on the work, activities, and people that give real meaning to my life. And yes, I love it."

ENDNOTES

INTRODUCTION

1. Thomas Johnson, Jr., "New York Life on Women's Retirement" (paper presented at WISER's Annual Symposium on Women's Retirement, December 2, 2010), accessed February 14, 2017.

2. "Tackling the Retirement Savings Gap," BlackRock, accessed February 14, 2017.

3. "How America Saves 2016," Vanguard 2015 Defined Contribution Plan Data, Vanguard, accessed February 14, 2017.

4. "2014 Wells Fargo Millennial Study," Wells Fargo, accessed February 2017.

5. Centers for Disease Control & Prevention, accessed February 14, 2017.

6. Benjamin Artz, Amanda H. Goodall, and Andrew J. Oswald "Do Women Ask?", Institute for the Study of Labor, accessed February 14, 2017.

7. Whitney Johnson, "Women, Finance the World You Want," Harvard Business Review, accessed February 14, 2017.

8. Bureau of Labor Statistics, 2009, accessed February 14, 2017.

9. UBS Investor Watch Report, "Couples and Money," 2014, accessed February 14, 2017.

10. "Tackling the Retirement Savings Gap," BlackRock, op.cit.

11. David Ronick, "The 5 Real Reasons Millennials Don't Invest," Stash, accessed February 14, 2017.

12. Belinda Luscombe, "Confidence Woman," *Time*, March 7, 2013, accessed February 14, 2017.

13. Suzanne McGee, "Sallie Krawcheck on her Wall Street ascent—and on how to 'attack the boys' club,'" *The Guardian*, August 28, 2016, accessed February 14, 2017.

14. Diana B. Elliott and Tavia Simmons, "Marital Events of Americans: 2009," United States Census Bureau, accessed February 14, 2017.

15. Mark Mather and Diana Lavery, "In U.S., Proportion Married at Lowest Recorded Levels," Population Reference Bureau, accessed February 14, 2017.

16. "Being a Woman Increases the Odds of Being Poor in America," National Women's Law Center, September 13, 2016, accessed February 14, 2017.

CHAPTER 1

1. "Are boys and girls equally prepared for life?" OECD Programme for International Student Assessment (PISA), 2014, accessed February 14, 2017.

2. Ibid.

3. "Vanguard Examines 401(k) Behavior/Outcome Gender Paradox," November 3, 2015, accessed February 14, 2017.

4. "Gender and Investing: Let's Set the Record Straight" SigFig, February 2015, accessed February 14, 2017.

CHAPTER 2

1. "Staying Invested During Volatile Markets," J.P. Morgan, Spring 2016, accessed February 14, 2017.

2. "Guru Grades," CXO Advisory, accessed February 14, 2017.

3. Claes Bell, "Did you miss the stock market rally? You're not alone," Bankrate.com, April 9, 2015, accessed February 14, 2017.

4. Brad M. Barber and Terrance Odean, "Boys Will Be Boys: Gender, Overconfidence and Common Stock Investment," *Quarterly Journal of Economics*, February 2001, p. 262, accessed February 14, 2017.

CHAPTER 3

1. Gary P. Brinson, L. Randolph Hood, and Gilbert L. Beebower, "Determinants of Portfolio Performance," *Financial Analysts Journal*, Vol. 42, No. 4 (July–August 1986), updated version accessed February 14, 2017.

CHAPTER 4

1. Source ©2017 Morningstar, Inc. All Rights Reserved.

2. "DALBAR Pinpoints Investor Pain" April 21, 2015, accessed February 14, 2017.

3. Eugene F. Fama and Kenneth R. French, "Luck versus Skill in the Cross-Section of Mutual Fund Returns," *The Journal of Finance*, Vol. LXV, No. 5, October 2010, p. 1, 916, accessed February 14, 2017.

4. Sam Ro, "The Past Performance of A Mutual Fund Is Not An Indicator of Future Outcomes . . . 96 Percent of The Time," *Business Insider*, July 13, 2014, accessed February 27, 2017.

5. "William Sharpe: an unsung hero of passive investing," Sensibleinvesting.tv, June 24, 2014, accessed February 14, 2017.

6. "Sauter: What lies ahead for indexing," Vanguard ETF Perspectives, Fall 2016, accessed February 27, 2017.

CHAPTER 7

1. Ashlea Ebeling, "The Search for Missing 401(k) Money," *Forbes*, August 27, 2013, accessed February 14, 2017.

2. "Tomorrow's Philanthropist," *Barclay's Wealth*, July 21, 2009, accessed February 14, 2017.

QUESTIONS TO CONSIDER
ASKING A FINANCIAL ADVISER

1. Who is the custodian of my investments?

2. What is the asset allocation you are using for my portfolio? What am I invested in? Am I invested internationally?

3. Are you a fee-only investment adviser, or are you a stockbroker? Please explain all the ways that you get paid when working with me. For example, in addition to the fees that I pay you directly, do you get paid in any way when you purchase investments for my account?

4. What are all the other fees and expenses I am paying? For example, how much am I paying other managers that you choose to manage my portfolios?

5 What is your investment philosophy? Do you believe that you or others can outperform the markets by actively picking certain stocks or by timing the markets?

6. What is/are the benchmarks that you are using to compare my portfolio returns to, and please explain why those are the correct benchmarks? How has my portfolio done against those benchmarks, and why?

7. If your investment adviser has selected outside managers for your accounts, how much turnover of the managers has there been?

8. What are the tax consequences of how you manage my investments? What percent annual turnover is there in the stocks that the underlying managers pick for my accounts?

GLOSSARY

ACTIVE MANAGEMENT:

A portfolio-management strategy where the fund manager deliberately picks and chooses specific investments with the goal of outperforming an investment benchmark (such as the S&P 500).

ASSET ALLOCATION:

The practice of dividing investments among different categories such as stocks, bonds, real estate, commodities, and cash equivalents to optimize the risk/reward tradeoff.

ASSET CLASSES:

A group of securities that exhibit similar characteristics. The main asset classes are:

- Stocks or equities
- Fixed income or bonds
- Money market or cash equivalents
- Real estate or other tangible assets
- Commodities

BENCHMARK:

The measure against which you compare your fund's returns to judge its performance. A benchmark can be the average performance of funds similar to yours or a broad index of the investments your fund usually picks from. The S&P 500 index is a good benchmark for funds that buy large-company stocks and the S&P Small Cap 600 is a good benchmark for small company stocks.

BONDS:

Bonds are loans. When you buy a bond, you become a lender to an institution. Your loan lasts a certain period of time—until the date when the bond reaches maturity—and you get a certain dividend payment each month (commonly known as a coupon) as interest on the loan. As long as the institution does not go bankrupt, it will also pay back the principal on the bond, but no more than the principal. There are two basic types of bonds: government bonds and corporate bonds. U.S. government bonds (otherwise known as T-bills or Treasuries) are issued and guaranteed by Uncle Sam. They typically offer a modest return with low risk. Corporate bonds are issued by companies and carry a higher degree of risk (should the company default) as well as return.

BROKER:

An investment executive or registered representative of a broker/dealer who specializes in selling various securities. A broker who sells stocks, bonds, and other securities must be registered in the province where the securities are traded. Broker-Dealers are "not to be deemed investment advisers" and therefore are not subject to the same fiduciary standards when recommending investments to clients, as are Registered Investment Advisers (RIAs). They are only required to recommend securities that are deemed "suitable" for clients.

Representatives of a Broker-Dealer who also engage in the business of providing investment advice are required to affiliate with an RIA. As Investment Adviser Representatives they are held to the Fiduciary Standard when providing investment advice to clients. This requires the dually registered Financial Advisers recommending a security to clearly communicate to their clients whether they are brokering a suitable security as a registered representative or providing investment advice as an Investment Adviser Representative and as such acting as a fiduciary.

CAPITALIZATION:

This describes the size of the company. It is the value of a company as measured by the total number of shares outstanding times the market price of each share. For example, if Apple Inc. has over 5.2 billion shares outstanding and each share is currently worth $137 per share, then the market capitalization for Apple is over $700 billion.

In general, stocks are classified as large cap (over $5 billion), small cap (under $2 billion), or mid cap (anything in between).

Mega cap: Over $200 billion (Apple, Microsoft, IBM)

Large cap: Over $5 billion (Staples)

Mid cap: $2 billion–$5 billion (Wendy's)

Small cap: $300 million–$2 billion (Pier 1; Shutterfly)

Micro cap: Below $300 million (Rosetta Stone)

COMPOUND INTEREST:

When you save or invest, your money can earn interest or appreciate. The next year, you can earn interest on your original money and on the interest (or appreciation) from the first year. In the third year, you earn interest on your original investment and also on the interest from the first two years. So, when interest is added to the principal, from that moment on, the interest that has been added also earns interest. This addition of interest to the principal is called compounding.

DEVELOPED INTERNATIONAL MARKETS:

Countries outside the United States that are considered developed include Australia, Austria, Belgium, Canada, Denmark, Finland, France, Germany, Greece, Hong Kong, Ireland, Israel, Italy, Japan, the Netherlands, New Zealand, Norway, Portugal, Singapore, Spain, Sweden, Switzerland, and the United Kingdom.

DIVERSIFICATION:

The practice of spreading money among different asset classes and geographic regions to reduce risk. Diversification is a strategy that can be neatly summed up by the timeless adage "Don't put all your eggs in one basket."

EMERGING MARKETS:

Countries with relatively young stock and bond markets such as Brazil, Chile, China, Colombia, the Czech Republic, Egypt, Hungary, India, Indonesia, Malaysia, Mexico, Peru, the Philippines, Poland, South Africa, South Korea, Taiwan, Thailand, and Turkey. Typically, emerging-markets investments have the potential for losses and gains larger than those of developed-market investments.

EQUITY/STOCK:

Ownership in a single company through the purchase of common shares or preferred shares (for example, shares in Apple or Starbucks). Unlike other assets, like bonds and cash, stocks represent a financial interest in businesses that may prove to be extremely profitable.

EXCHANGE-TRADED FUND:

An exchange-traded fund (ETF) describes the broad class of funds, excluding closed-end funds, that trade throughout the day on an exchange. These funds can track a variety of stock, bond, commodity, real estate, and currency indexes. ETFs do not need to redeem shares for cash, and thus do not need to sell securities (possibly realizing capital gains) to pay investors who redeem their shares. They are typically more tax-efficient than mutual funds as they have fewer trades and lower portfolio turnover. Most ETFs are index funds. ETFs have gained favor because of their low expenses, tax efficiency, diversification, transparency, trading flexibility, and intraday liquidity. ETFs have low annual expenses (expense ratio) and the investor usually pays a commission to trade them. Diversification is an attractive feature of ETFs. Instead of taking concentrated risks by purchasing individual stocks, investors can own an index of stocks with ETFs.

EXPENSE RATIO:

The annual fee that all funds or ETFs charge their shareholders. It expresses the percentage of assets deducted each fiscal year for fund expenses, including 12b-1 fees, management fees, administrative fees, operating costs, and all other asset-based costs incurred by the fund.

FIDUCIARY:

A fiduciary, such as PowerHouse Assets, is subject to the highest duty of care to its clients under law. While I believe that all financial service providers should act as fiduciaries, unfortunately, most do not. A fiduciary must always put the best interests of the client first.

FIXED INCOME SECURITIES:

Fixed income securities pay a fixed rate of return in the form of interest or dividend income. Examples include bonds and preferred shares.

GROWTH STOCK/FUND:

A growth-oriented fund will hold the stocks of companies that the portfolio manager believes will increase earnings faster than the rest of the market.

INDEX FUND:

A fund designed to mirror the performance of a specific market index such as the Dow Jones Industrial Average or the S&P 500. Expenses of index funds tend to be lower than other mutual funds because the manager is not actively researching, buying, and selling securities. Index funds are considered to be passively managed because the portfolio manager of each index fund is replicating the index, rather than trading securities based on his or her view of the potential risk/reward characteristics of various securities. Conversely, an actively managed fund has a portfolio manager who is buying and selling securities based on an opinion about which securities will accomplish the fund's objectives. An S&P 500 index fund is a passively managed fund that mimics the S&P 500 index.

INFLATION:

A persistent increase in the level of consumer prices or a persistent decline in the purchasing power of money, caused by an increase in available currency and credit beyond the proportion of available goods and services.

LARGE-CAP STOCK:

A large-cap stock refers to almost the same thing as large company stock. A company's capitalization is the total value of all its stock—that is, the price of a company's stock times the number of shares it has sold. Large-cap companies are usually very big corporations, like Exxon, Apple, IBM, or Microsoft.

MUTUAL FUND:

A fund that invests in a group of assets in accordance with one or more stated objectives, such as income, growth, or aggressive

growth. A mutual fund may generally invest in stocks, bonds, options, futures, currencies, and money market securities in accordance with its stated parameters. Most mutual funds, other than
index funds, use active management, though different managers
use different methods to pick their investments. Active management is the opposite of passive management, or indexing. Fees
are higher for active management. All shareholders share equally
in the income, gains, and losses generated by the fund.

PASSIVE INVESTING/INDEX INVESTING:

Investing in a fund that tracks a market index, such as the S&P
Index. Because passive funds mirror the performance of a particular index, the performance numbers are very similar to the
index. Management fees are considerably lower for index-based
mutual funds.

PASSIVELY MANAGED FUND:

A passively managed fund is a fund whose investment securities
are not specifically chosen by a portfolio manager, but instead
are selected to match an index or part of the market. This is the
opposite of an actively managed fund.

PORTFOLIO:

The term used for all the securities owned by an individual,
an institutional investor, or a mutual fund portfolio manager.
A portfolio may contain a combination of investments, such as
stocks, bonds, and other securities.

REAL ESTATE INVESTMENT TRUST:

Known as REITs, these vehicles invest in a portfolio of real estate properties—often commercial or apartment buildings. REITs are modeled after mutual funds, although the tax treatment of REIT income is different.

REBALANCING:

Bringing your portfolio back to your original asset-allocation mix. This is necessary because over time some of your investments may become out of alignment with your investment goals. You'll find that some of your investments will grow faster than others. By rebalancing, you'll ensure that your portfolio does not overemphasize one or more asset categories, and you'll return your portfolio to a comfortable level of risk.

REGISTERED INVESTMENT ADVISER (RIA):

An investment adviser who is registered either with the Securities and Exchange Commission or a state's securities agency. In general, Registered Investment Advisers managing assets totaling less than $100 million must register with the state securities agency in the state where they have their principal place of business. Registration of an investment adviser is a legal requirement and does not imply any level of skill or training.

S&P 500 INDEX:

The Standard & Poor's index of 500 stocks is a popular standard for measuring stock market performance among the biggest, most broadly based companies in the US. The S&P 500 represents about 80 percent of the value of US publicly traded companies.

SMALL-CAP STOCK:

Typically new or relatively young companies that have a market cap between $100 million to $2 billion. Small-capitalization companies do present the possibility of greater capital appreciation and are inherently a greater risk.

TURNOVER RATIO:

This is the percentage of stocks that a fund manager sells in a portfolio or mutual fund in a given year.

VALUE STOCK/FUND:

A value-oriented fund contains stocks that are currently undervalued in price-to-earnings or price-to-book value.

ACKNOWLEDGMENTS

Since I have always been a numbers person, writing this book took a village. For their advice, encouragement and help, I am deeply grateful to:

Suzanne McGee, my writer, without whom I'd still be staring at a blank computer screen. With her wealth of knowledge and expertise in the financial industry, we were able to talk in shorthand with each other. She turned ideas into written words, outlines into chapters.

Brooke Carey, who in a short period of time applied her fantastic editorial talent to shape and edit the manuscript into a strong and coherent narrative.

The team at Regan Arts: Judith Regan—for believing in the book from the start, as well as Lucas Wittmann, Kathryn Huck, Lynne Ciccaglione, Richard Ljoenes, and Nancy Singer, who brought the project from manuscript to book in record time.

Laine Morreau, for expertly copyediting the manuscript.

Sandi Mendelson, who has guided me with her insightful perspective and wisdom, and the team at Hilsinger Mendelson for helping to spread the word about the book's mission.

The brilliant and wonderful people at Dimensional Fund

Advisors: Jamie Norman, who helped me with the data sources for the charts; Iwona Hill and Kahne Krause, who started the Women's Wealth Initiatives, and brought together like-minded women in the independent financial industry who share the same investment philosophy, and are dynamic, generous, empathetic and dedicated to their clients: Cammie Doder, Chiara Renninger, Diane Bourdo, Eileen O'Connor, Evelyn Zohlen, Gretchen Halpin, Heather Locus, Heather Hooper, Kimberly Foss, Laura Jansen, Lorna Hallenbeck, Manisha Thakor, Mary Harris, Neela Hummel, Rachel Robasciotti, Sharon Allen, Stacy Francis, and Stuart Smith.

My friends who are authors or have experience in this industry, who gave me their expert advice and support: Deborah Weisgall, Zac Bissonette, Beth Wechsler, Janet Silver, Robyn Roth, Ruth Nemzoff, and Ed McLaughlin.

Janey Bishoff, the consummate, dedicated professional with the utmost integrity with whom I always look forward to working.

Matina Horner, whom I had the great fortune of having as a mentor in college. With good humor and wisdom, you have been a model for me and generations of women, showing us how to balance it all and live life to the fullest.

Andrea Jung, an inspiring role model both when she was at Avon and now at Grameen America where she is improving many women's lives.

My clients (both men and women), and the women who have participated in PowerHouses who inspire and motivate me. I am constantly learning from their questions.

And always, my love and immense appreciation for my family and friends who have lived through the whole publishing process with me, encouraged me, and served as invaluable sounding boards: Dave Wazer, Kaylee Finn-Henry, Michael Finn-Henry, Caroline Wazer, Annie Wazer, Lois Finn, Ruth Finn Oshin, Eliot Finn, Robin Zhang, Alexa Oshin, Matthew Oshin, Harris Berman, Debby Finn, Alyssa Finn, Lisa Vinikoor, Carolyn Finn, Leonard Finn, Sarah Finn, Julie Finn, Alana Zion-Buchalla, Laura Barone, Rali Tufts, Renata Villers, Brizio Biondi-Morra, Phil Villers, Charlie and Sharon Ross, Anne Hulecki, Jonathan Slater, Laurie Endlar Lee, Carol Pastan Lazar, Laurie Smith, Nancy Kelley, Peter Green, Judith Praitis, Mitra and Piran Sioshansi, Ronald and Kathryn Heifetz, Tom Risser, Edie McKay, Robin Kornegay-Rougeau, Vince Rougeau, Susan Kahn, Wendi Daniels, Beverly Weinfeld, Barbara McLaughlin, Mark Jung, Steve Gordon, Lauri Union, Mark Feinstein, Chip Johns, and Dan Ginsburg.

Finally, I thank the readers who I hope will share their knowledge with others so together we can transform how women think about investing for our futures.

INDEX

CREDITS

or guarantees the accuracy of completeness of any information or material contained herin, nor do they make any warranty, express or implied, as to the results to be obtained therefrom. To the maximum extent allowed by law, neither Bloomberg nor Barclays shall have any liability or responsibility for injury or damages arising in connection therewith.

BofA Merrill Lynch index data is used by permission, Copyright © Bank of America Corporation ("BAC"). The use of the above in no way implies that BAC or any of its affiliates endorses the view or interpretation or the use of such information or acts as any endorsement of the author's use of such information. The information is provided "as is" and none of BAC or any of its affiliates warrants the accuracy or completeness of the information.

Citigroup Index LLC (Citi) makes no representation as to the accuracy, adequacy, or completeness of the Citi data and is not responsible for any errors or omissions or for the results obtained from its use.

ABOUT THE AUTHOR

Alice Finn is a wealth management expert. She was featured as "The Giant" by Barron's in its inaugural list of the Top 100 Independent Financial Advisers, and she has appeared as a top financial adviser on CNBC. Alice has also been named repeatedly by *Worth Magazine* as one of the Top 100 Wealth Advisers in the United States. She is the CEO of PowerHouse Assets LLC, a firm she founded to help women become more engaged in their important financial futures. Prior to that, Finn was cofounder, CEO, and Chief Investment Officer of Ballentine, Finn, and Company Inc., ranked #1 Wealth Manager by Bloomberg, where she grew the firm's assets under advisement to $5 billion. Under her leadership, the firm was consistently named by Charles Schwab as among the industry's best-managed firms. Finn is a Certified Financial Planner (CFP), has an AB from Harvard, a MALD from The Fletcher School at Tufts, and a JD from Harvard Law School.